D0120335

Homes in Britain

HOMES
IN BRITAIN

From the Earliest Times to 1900

AUDREY BARFOOT

B. T. BATSFORD LTD LONDON

First published 1963
Third impression 1969

MADE AND PRINTED IN GREAT BRITAIN BY
WILLIAM CLOWES AND SONS LTD, LONDON AND BECCLES
FOR THE PUBLISHERS
B. T. BATSFORD LTD
4 FITZHARDINGE STREET, PORTMAN SQUARE, LONDON W.I

Contents

Introduction

FROM THE EARLIEST days of his existence, man has needed shelter from the weather and prowling wild beasts. Because of the perishable nature of primitive man's building materials, details of his early life are largely a matter of conjecture, but much may be learned from archaeologists' expert and patient research.

We can trace man's progress from purely functional caves and hovels, through a brief interlude of Roman civilization succeeded by bigger hovels, to dwellings of comfort and elegance. It is easy to condemn the living-conditions of the past by applying our own standards of comfort and taste; it should, however, be remembered that, in early days, people knew of no such standards, so that life was tolerable to them, and should be judged in the context of the age.

Even today there are slums, overcrowding and homeless people, and man has still to achieve universally ideal living-conditions. Much has been done; much remains to be done.

Detailed reference to palaces, castles and famous 'stately homes' is not within the scope of this book. Actual dates of construction are quoted when they are known; approximate dates are prefaced by 'c.' from the Latin 'circa'—meaning 'about'.

The author wishes to acknowledge the great deal of help given to her by the publishers of this book.

Note: The numbers in parentheses in the text refer to the page-numbers of the illustrations.

1 Prehistoric and Pre-Roman Britain

CAVE PAINTING

OUR EARLIEST, Palaeolithic, ancestors probably lived in trees. They were nomadic hunters with no permanent homes. Their successors, Mesolithic, or Middle Stone Age, people (12,000 B.C. onwards) used fire for warmth, primitive cooking and protection from wild beasts. They lived in caves, and sometimes decorated the walls with paintings of animals.

By about 10,000 B.C. the Ice Age was ending; the polar icecap had receded, glaciers had melted and the climate was gradually becoming milder. Bleak tundra slowly became forests. Middle Stone Age men were still nomadic hunters and herdsmen, needing no permanent homes, and probably constructed temporary shelters of branches, bark and skins over shallow pits scraped in light soil (**9**).

During the Late Stone Age (3,000–1,850 B.C.) more permanent dwellings were evolved, shaped like a modern bell-tent, about 20–25 feet in diameter. The drawing opposite has been 'cut away' to show the interior construction of a shallow pit surrounded by poles which were inserted in a circular bank of earth (to prevent spreading and consequent collapse); these were interlaced with twigs to form a rough hurdle and fixed to a central pole, the whole being covered with bracken, heather and turf. It was entered by a low hole in the wall, which could be closed to intruders, man or beast, by a bundle of brushwood or an uprooted gorse-bush.

Farming and agriculture had developed by the Bronze Age (1,850–550 B.C.). Families and tribes made settlements surrounded by raised defensive earthworks. Thus, village life began. The Bronze Age dwelling (**9**), based on archaeological researches made on Dartmoor, shows how a circular bank of earth, reinforced with stones, was built higher to give increased head-room; there was a raised sleeping platform and a rough porch. The centre and radiating poles remained.

The stone 'beehive' hut, considered to be typical of this period, in rocky districts where timber was not readily available, is similar to summer *sheilings* built in the Hebrides during the 19th century; ruins of earlier examples have been discovered in Wales, Cornwall and the West Country.

The Iron Age (550 B.C.–A.D. 43) house illustrated opposite could accommodate 30 people or a whole household, farmyard animals and stores. The enclosed cattle-stalls follow the principle of domestic animals living with the family. Mainly timber construction was common in fertile, wooded districts such as southern Britain. The smoke from the central hearth escaped through the apex of the coarsely thatched roof by means of a flue made of poles and hurdles. There were two interior circles of poles, the outer circle being used as cattle-stalls or possibly sleeping-cubicles for human inhabitants.

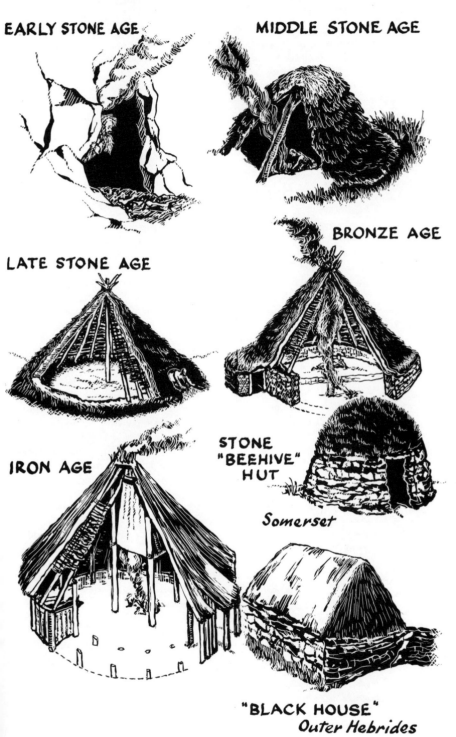

EARLY STONE AGE

MIDDLE STONE AGE

LATE STONE AGE

BRONZE AGE

IRON AGE

STONE "BEEHIVE" HUT

Somerset

"BLACK HOUSE"
Outer Hebrides

9

The rectangular 'Black House' (**9**), of comparatively recent construction in the Hebrides, accommodated both humans and cattle. It was built of stone with a roughly thatched roof supported on poles.

Excavations in Cornwall have revealed complicated patterns of *hut-clusters* comprising circular houses, oval byres and long, narrow storerooms, possibly for fodder.

2 *Roman Britain* A.D. 43–410

FOLLOWING JULIUS CAESAR'S two reconnaissance expeditions in 55 and 54 B.C., the Romans invaded Britain in A.D. 43 and within four years the conquest and colonization of the south-east were virtually complete. Good roads and walled cities were established. Wealthier folk's houses were comfortable and elegant, with separate rectangular rooms, pillared corridors, tiled floors often with mosaic pavements, efficient plumbing and under-floor heating. Peasants in poor, remote and unconquered districts retained their wattle huts.

The drawing opposite shows a Roman-British villa with an upper floor; many villas were of the bungalow type. Walls were constructed of stone, bricks and durable mortar, or *wattle and daub* (hurdles plastered on to a timber framework with clay and straw), and finally finished with smooth, coloured plaster. Roofs were of tiles or stone slates. Usually the ground-floor plan of a villa included a number of small rooms leading off an *atrium* or large, central living-room, a *triclinium* or dining room, women's apartments, a shrine to the gods, a bathroom and servants' quarters.

'Central heating' was by *hypocaust*. In an underground furnace-room were brick pillars supporting the ground floor and allowing heat to circulate, and hollow tiles in the walls conducted the warm air through the house, small trails of smoke escaping under the eaves.

Good plumbing and baths were customary; windows were glazed with thick glass. Kitchens were well equipped with brick or stone charcoal-ovens and cooking utensils. There were comfortable wooden beds, couches, tables and stools, elegant pottery, bronze and iron candlesticks, etc.

A LAR

(Household god)

In non-Christian households, a small altar was dedicated to the household gods, *lares et penates*. The *lar familiaris*, god of the freehold, had to be greeted, worshipped and presented with offerings. The *penates* presided over family property.

When the Romans left Britain, it was invaded by barbarian hordes, who burned, sacked and pillaged cities, destroying the high standard of Roman civilization. Thus, Britain returned to further centuries of cold, comfortless living, and the 'Dark Ages' descended.

ROMAN-BRITISH VILLA
Exterior

Hollow tiles

GROUND FLOOR

HYPOCAUST
Furnace

ROMAN-BRITISH VILLA
Interior

3 The Dark Ages and the Saxons 410–1066

AFTER THE ROMANS had left Britain it fell easily to invading Picts, and Teutonic Angles, Jutes and Saxons who became predominant. Surviving Roman-British cities and homesteads were left to decay, and new settlements were established elsewhere. Whole communities lived a truly communal life in one large 'hall' (**13**).

1962

Being skilled shipwrights, the Saxons did not build houses of stone or brick, but timber dwellings resembling inverted ship-hulls, whose wooden ribs were shaped with adzes when the natural curve of trees could not be utilized. Often they followed the prehistoric custom of digging a hole and resting the roof on ground level, so that a house was 'all roof and no wall'. A 'Vacation Home' in a recent Ideal Home Exhibition is of this construction.

The construction of a Saxon house can be seen in the 'cut-away' drawing opposite which shows ribs, ridge-pole at the top of the roof, *wattle and daub*, all covered in turf or rough thatch. Rafters and buttresses made vertical supports unnecessary, thus clearing floor-space. Main arched timbers were called *crucks*.

In humbler halls, cattle were stalled in an *outshot* or *bays* by inside walls. Where the owner could afford separate byres, granaries and stables, people slept either on the hall floor of beaten earth covered with rushes (and rubbish), or in bunk-beds built against the wall and sheltered, perhaps, by curtains or wooden shutters (**13**).

Smoke from the central hearth filtered through a hole in the roof. The general draughts, smoke, dirt, vermin and lack of privacy would have horrified a Roman landowner. Spluttering torches dipped in fat replaced Roman lamps and candles. Furniture was clumsy and rough-hewn; there were no baths or drainage. Glass in windows was a forgotten luxury; they were sometimes shielded with strips of horn, but were usually narrow and closed with shutters.

By the end of this period a pattern of society had developed, the beginning of the *feudal system*. Groups of *villeins* were subject to an overlord or *thane*; he lived in his hall, surrounded by out-buildings including a *bur* for the women (the beginning of privacy), kitchen, chapel, dovecote and farm-buildings, all defended by a ditch and timber stockade, surrounded by peasants' hovels.

WORDS OF SAXON ORIGIN

Bay—cattle stall in hall

Bur—women's room. Hence 'bower'

Feld—clearing in forest. Hence place-names Lingfield, Uckfield, etc.

First—ridge-pole of roof

Ham—water-meadow

Lea—meadow

Rod, pole or *perch*—unit of measurement in building, 16 feet being the width of a *bay* for 4 oxen, or 16 men's right feet placed one behind the other

Tun—farm

Tunscripe—group of farms. Hence 'township'

AXON HOUSES

Ground level

Interior Construction

"Teapot Hall" Lincolnshire

A SAXON HALL

4 Norman and 'Transitional' 1066-1200

BY THE NORMAN CONQUEST, the Saxons had developed townships consisting mainly of single-storied houses separated by narrow lanes, and defended with earthworks, ditches and timber stockades against Danish invaders. Houses were still made of timber, and Saxon builders gradually discovered how to construct vertical walls, as opposed to the 'all roof, no wall' technique (13). This was an obvious advantage where houses were close together in towns. Maybe ruins of Roman-British villas had inspired them. Horizontal *tie-beams* or *baulks*, supported at the junction of walls and roof, crossed communal living-quarters from side to side; some enterprising householders laid planks across these beams (except where smoke drifted through the roof from the central hearth), thus forming a loft for storing grain or hay, or even—daring innovation—for sleeping-quarters. So began the upper floor.

To conquer and finally unite Britain involved far more than winning the Battle of Hastings. Admittedly the Saxons were primarily a farming people, inclined to be easy-going as opposed to the disciplined Normans. However, any risings were ruthlessly put down, and during the early years of the Conquest it is logically assumed that quickly-erected timber dwellings were used, while large stone castles were gradually built. Priority was given to defence and security, and comfort came a bad second. As military necessity became less pressing, living-standards improved.

The Normans developed and thoroughly organized the feudal system; estates or *manors* (from the French *manoir*) were granted to powerful nobles, complete with serfs, mostly conquered Saxons, bound to farm their lord's land. These peasants continued to live in squalor, their *wattle and daub* huts huddled round the castle of their Lord of the Manor (15). Smoke from the central hearth still drifted through sooty and leaking thatch; cattle still shared the householders' communal living-room.

After some years of peace, the wealthier Saxons' knowledge of building was allied to Norman improvements, and houses were built with an upper floor or *solar* (probably derived from the same root as the French *solive*, a floor-joist, and *entresol*, a mezzanine floor). Originally, the word *solar* meant the upper floor-boards, but it was subsequently used to denote an upper room. Stone was increasingly used in house-building, although timber houses were more common than is often supposed; however, only those of more durable material have survived (17). It is probable that an existing Saxon hall was retained for servants, while the Normans, disliking communal squalor, built their own adjacent quarters.

With the introduction of the *solar*, a central hearth was impracticable, so fireplaces were moved to a recess in a thick side-wall, the smoke escaping through holes in a hollow buttress outside, an early form of flue. Examples of this device may be found in early Norman keeps at the Tower of London, Rochester Castle and Castle Hedingham in Essex. By the late 12th century, tall chimney-stacks were invented, as may still be seen in the ruins of Christchurch Castle (15).

Internal access to early *solars* was by means of a ladder and opening in

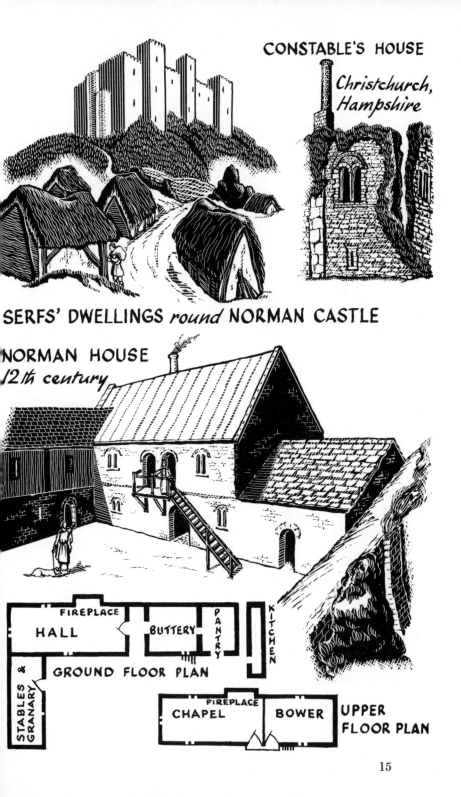

CONSTABLE'S HOUSE

Christchurch, Hampshire

SERFS' DWELLINGS *round* NORMAN CASTLE

NORMAN HOUSE
12th century

FIREPLACE

HALL

BUTTERY

PANTRY

KITCHEN

GROUND FLOOR PLAN

STABLES & GRANARY

FIREPLACE

CHAPEL

BOWER

UPPER FLOOR PLAN

the wooden floor. Where later houses had more than one upper room, an external wooden staircase and small balcony, called an *oriel*, were built (**15**), leading from a central courtyard.

The plan of the 12th-century Norman manor house (**15**) included a large hall, still the focal point of daily life, where the noble lord and his family

FIREPLACE

dined at a long refectory table on a raised dais placed comfortably out of draughts, and the serfs fed 'below the salt' (**17**). The lofty, beamed roof here illustrated indicates that this hall was either on an upper floor over storerooms, similar in construction to the Norman Hall at Boothby Pagnell, or extending from the ground floor to the roof of the upper floor. The floor was strewn with rushes (and remains of food, scavenged by dogs), and high, unglazed windows were either open to the weather or covered with thin strips of horn. Walls might be adorned with tapestries, and light was provided by spluttering torches resting in iron *sconces* or brackets.

Next to the hall were the *buttery* or wine-store (from the French *bouteille*, bottle) and pantry (from the French *pain*, bread). The kitchen, a thatched lean-to, was still built apart from the rest of the house because of fire-hazard.

The women's upper-floor *bower* provided them with some privacy from the noise and roistering in the hall, and could also be used as sleeping-quarters.

Fireplaces were made more imposing and less smoky by chimney-hoods (**17**). Roofs were covered either with lead or with stone tiles.

By the late 12th century, vaulted basement rooms or *undercrofts* were constructed for storage. Beautiful examples of rooms below ground-level may be seen in the Close by Winchester Cathedral. The example illustrated opposite, from the Angel Inn, Guildford, is, in fact, of the thirteenth century and shows, in its pointed window-openings and vaulting, the increasing influence of the continental Gothic style. This began to appear in England during the second half of the century, and by the beginning of the thirteenth century the transition from Norman to Early English Gothic (see page **18**) was almost complete. The architecture during this period is, appropriately, called 'Transitional'.

VAULTED BASEMENT
Guildford, Surrey

NORMAN HALL
Boothby Pagnell, Lincolnshire

CHIMNEY HOOD
Boothby Pagnell

Interior of
NORMAN HALL

5 The Middle Ages 1200–1500

SAXON SKILL ALLIED to the Normans' more sophisticated knowledge of building gradually evolved the grace and beauty of the Early English, or first period of Gothic architecture, a style which produced such glorious buildings as the eastern end of Westminster Abbey. This style was reflected in the houses of prosperous folk of the period. Except in the north and on the Welsh Marches, where it was found necessary to maintain fortified manor houses for defensive purposes, each with its watch-tower, keep, thick walls and narrow slit-windows, life became much more comfortable and homely.

Opposite are illustrated examples of 13th-century domestic architecture. The hall, often built over a vaulted basement or *undercroft* (**17**), remained the principal room and focal point of life in a manor house of this period, which was usually built of stone with a lead or tiled roof. It was a long, lofty room, extending in height from the ground floor to the roof of the upper floor, and thus cutting off from each other any upper rooms at opposite ends of the house, which had separate staircases. The ceiling of the hall was of timber. Early English builders had mastered the art of constructing massive *principals* or wooden arches to support rafters and longitudinal beams or *purlins*, without the need of vertical pillars which were an advanced form of the Saxon *cruck* (**13**). Timber roofs grew more graceful and elaborate as the Middle Ages progressed (**19, 21, 23**). The householder ate, with his family and any guests, at the 'high table' on a dais in the hall.

KITCHEN c. 1400

His servants and retainers fed at long tables 'below the salt' as in Norman times (**17**). At the other end were the pantry and buttery, their entrances concealed by screens or *speers* of carved wood with no doors. The kitchen was built separately from the main part of the house. The hall floor was still covered with rushes—and by layers of garbage, which caused the Dutch scholar Erasmus to remark, even in the early years of the 16th century, that rushes were 'so renewed that the substratum may be unmolested for twenty years, with an ancient collection of beer, grease, fragments, bones, spittle and everything that is nasty'.

Although the whole household might still eat and sleep in the hall, attention to family privacy was increasing and the *solar* was commonly built over storerooms. In this way the head of the family could keep a vigilant eye on his stores, as well as having a room to which he could retire from the noise and dirt of the hall (**21**). The *solar* was also called the *withdrawing-room*; hence our modern term 'drawing-room'. Its wooden floor was strewn with woven rugs brought from the East by returning Crusaders. The stone walls were either left bare, or plastered and decorated with painted lines and simple patterns, or hung with tapestries.

As can be seen from the plan (**19**), a small chapel was a customary part of a manor house.

Hygiene had slightly improved, and a sanitary wing was added. This

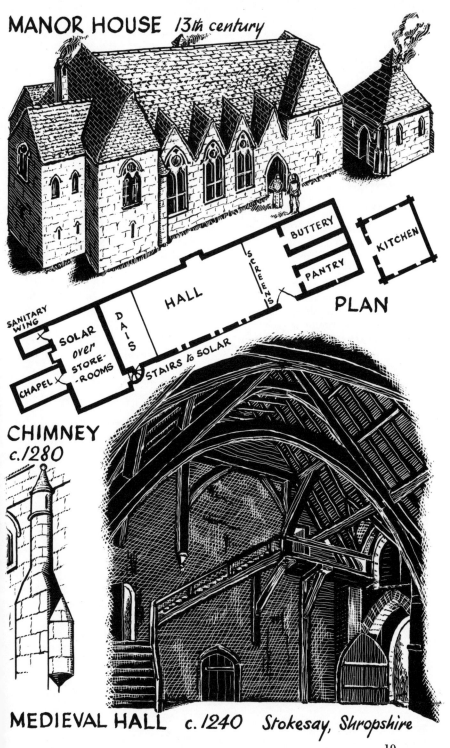

MANOR HOUSE *13th century*

BUTTERY

KITCHEN

SCREENS

PANTRY

HALL

PLAN

SANITARY WING

DAIS

SOLAR over STORE-ROOMS

STAIRS to SOLAR

CHAPEL

CHIMNEY
c.1280

MEDIEVAL HALL   c.1240   *Stokesay, Shropshire*

provided facilities for washing and even baths, said to have been introduced into England by Eleanor of Castile, wife of King Edward I. However, baths were generally considered an eccentric luxury, and not a necessity. There was, of course, no plumbing or running water; servants would toil up and down with buckets of water drawn from the nearest well and heated in the kitchen. In this wing was also a *garde-robe, privy* or lavatory, which worked on the earth-closet principle.

Although some medieval builders continued to construct a central hearth in the hall, this had become old-fashioned, and fire-places were usually built in the thickness of the wall. Conservative architects clung to the buttress-flue (**19**), although tall chimneys had been introduced during the previous period. Where chimneys were built, they were often decorated (**21**).

A minstrels' gallery, approached by an internal staircase in the hall, was becoming popular (**19**).

Windows, built in thick walls, were equipped with recessed window-seats (**21**) and often protected with iron bars and wooden shutters. Panes of glass were not yet in general use, a little, expensively imported from France, being mainly put into churches or nobles' castles. Windows were either open to the weather or covered with thin strips of horn; apparently a medieval householder could not have both light and warmth in cold weather. The gatehouse shown opposite, originally a defence by a moat now filled in, is an example of 14th-century (the Decorated period of Gothic architecture) half-timber and plaster construction. External beams are usually assumed to be typical of 16th-century Tudor architecture, and so they were, but this type of construction had been introduced much earlier, and

FARMHOUSE
15th century

built on to an improved *wattle and daub* foundation. An example of this may be seen in The King's Head at Aylesbury.

By the 15th century the Perpendicular period of Gothic architecture had reached great heights of elegance and comfort. The plan of the manor house (**23**) indicates that a prosperous householder had really achieved

privacy apart from the communal life of the hall, if he desired it. As far as living-standards were concerned, there was no middle class as we know it; people were either wealthy, powerful and comfortable, or poverty-stricken in squalid conditions. But a small social revolution was taking place; people, other than the nobility, were making fortunes from the wool trade, and independent yeomen-farmers were rising from the ranks of the agricultural peasantry.

While the lofty hall, with its elaborate timbered roof (**23**), still dominated house-construction, the family could take their meals in a separate *dining-parlour* if they desired, and retire to their *winter-parlour*. The *solar* could be used as a bedroom, and the *great chamber* or principal bedroom, complete with its four-poster bed, was added. These innovations were not popular with the servants and retainers. Besides the extra housework involved, they probably resented the fact that the upper classes were breaking away from the completely communal life of their forefathers, and considered that they were becoming increasingly aloof and snobbish.

SOLAR or WITHDRAWING ROOM c. 1290

WINDOW
14th century

CHIMNEY
14th century

Herefordshire 14th century

21

The dais, for ceremonial dining, and the minstrels' gallery remained features of the hall.

Garde-robes or latrines were provided.

The kitchen, with its rear courtyard, was now included in the plan of the house.

Houses were constructed of stone or timber, but, towards the end of the 14th century, bricks, unknown in Britain since Roman times, were accidentally imported from Flanders as ballast in returning wool-ships. By the end of the 15th century bricks were being made in England and used for house-building.

Roofs were covered with lead or tiles.

In half-timbered houses (**25**) the main horizontal beam was sometimes elaborately carved. Windows projected and were, by this time, glazed with small leaded panes. A city street typical of crowded London, by then the thronged centre of trade and commerce, shows how lath-and-plaster houses were packed closely together along narrow streets, their high gables jutting out at crazy angles and almost touching their opposite neighbours. It is no wonder that the Great Plague followed by the Fire of London ravaged the City in the 17th century.

Details of medieval building are shown on page **25**.

A more graceful fireplace replaced the cumbersome *chimney-hood* and could be decorated with the owner's armorial bearings if he were entitled to them.

In early medieval houses windows were small, particularly on the ground floor, because of the need for defence; but as the times became more peaceful windows grew larger and more decorated. During the 15th century, large bay windows were built on the ground floor in the graceful Perpendicular style. From the walls of the upper floors projected *oriel windows*. This term, previously used to denote small balconies built on Norman houses (**15**), was probably derived from the French word *oreille*, ear.

No prosperous medieval farm, particularly an ecclesiastical one, was complete without its dovecote or *culver-house*, a term derived from the obsolete word *culver*, a dove or pigeon. These birds were a substantial item of medieval diet, but caused great damage to crops and were much resented by the peasantry as only lords of the manor, monastic orders and parochial clergy were allowed to keep them. The dovecotes were large and well built in stone with thick walls, apparently much better than the hovels of poor agricultural peasants.

Having turned from city streets to the countryside, one may well enquire after the welfare of the peasantry and farming communities. Theirs was a hard lot; true, by the 13th and 14th centuries, farming methods had improved, and the villeins, or serfs bound to their lord under the *feudal system*, were gradually becoming more free in that it had become customary for rent to be exacted for their holdings of land in lieu of their labour and produce. With the increase of sheep-farming, which needed fewer labourers than agriculture, a villein might purchase his freedom and could travel about, hiring himself to various farmers. Manor farms were self-supporting. This was all very well for enterprising and go-ahead types, but those who were not free to lead a nomadic existence, taking work where they found

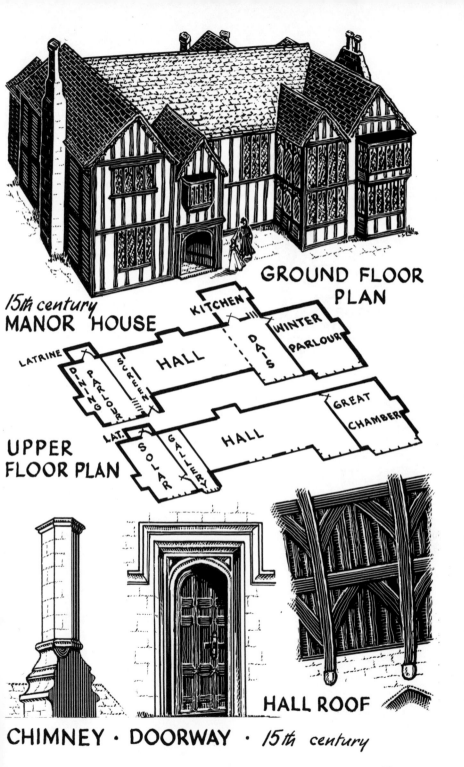

GROUND FLOOR PLAN

15th century MANOR HOUSE

KITCHEN

WINTER PARLOUR

DAIS

LATRINE

DINING PARLOUR

SCREEN

HALL

GREAT CHAMBER

UPPER FLOOR PLAN

LAT.

SOLAR

GALLERY

HALL

HALL ROOF

CHIMNEY · DOORWAY · *15th century*

it, fell into dire poverty and misery when they were dispossessed of their small plots of land. The poorest farm labourers still lived in squalor, in huts little better than those of their Saxon forbears (**13**). In 1348–9 life was made harder by the ravages of the Black Death, an epidemic of plague which swept through the land, killing off about half the entire population. Consequently, for some years there were too few labourers left to cultivate the land properly, and this gave an added impetus to sheep-farming. The scarcity of labour might increase the wages of a lucky few, but they could

PIQUE CANDLESTICKS

not demand such increase as a right. The new classes of wealthy wool-merchants and independent yeoman-farmers wanted a house better than a peasant's hut, though not as grand and costly as a manor. They modelled their modest homes on the plans of manor houses, and an early 16th-century dwelling in this category is illustrated in the next chapter.

LIGHTING

Early Medieval: Rush lights dipped in oil and held in an iron clip, or torches.

Fifteenth-century: Soft wax or tallow candles impaled on *piques* or iron spikes, either singly or grouped on an iron circle.

15th century

FIREPLACE
Dorset

HALF-TIMBERING *Essex*

DOVECOTE

Herefordshire

ORIEL
WINDOW
Dorset

A CITY STREET

25

6 The Sixteenth Century

OVEN

THE YEAR 1500 marks the close of the Middle Ages, and the beginning of the Renaissance or 'Rebirth of learning'. Great advances in scholarship, the creative arts of music, painting and literature (the latter being spread more widely and speedily by the invention of printing) and interest in Classical architecture were being made and were spreading throughout Europe. England was emerging from backward, medieval insularity and was taking her place among the more culturally advanced European countries.

As described in Chapter 2, the military power and civilizing influence of Rome had collapsed in the 5th century, and Britain relapsed into the barbarism of the Dark Ages. Yet Roman culture was not quite dead, and gradually, throughout subsequent centuries, Italian influence percolated through the rest of Europe, due largely to Christian missionaries. Successive Popes came to exercise enormous influence over western Europe, and the Church gained great power, both spiritual and temporal. Classical and Italian architecture, both ecclesiastical and secular, had a marked effect on almost all forms of building, first in France, Germany and the Low Countries where Italian styles were modified and mingled with various national characteristics; finally the new ideas of the Renaissance, not only pure Italian but also French and Dutch, reached England. Various details of Renaissance influence are shown in subsequent illustrations, and also something of the wide variety of styles in stone, brick and timber.

'Tudor' architecture is automatically associated with beams and half-timbering (hence modern versions of 'Mock Tudor'), but half-timbering and plaster were an established style by the 14th century (21). Fifteenth- and 16th-century architects elaborated and improved timber-framed houses, and Tudor craftsmen, combining beams with beautifully intricate brickwork, reached glorious standards. As in the study of historic costume, it must not be imagined that some dramatic change in styles happened overnight with the accession of the first Tudor sovereign, Henry VII, in 1485. Each period of history merges gradually into the next epoch or century.

Both national and international events had marked repercussions on the domestic life of the time. Henry VIII's quarrel with the Pope, arising from his matrimonial problems, led to the Reformation, and the Dissolution of the Monasteries, from 1536 onwards, meant that much land and many buildings were taken out of ecclesiastical hands and passed into secular ones, giving increased scope for house-building. While this may have temporarily decreased the popularity of purely Italian influence, the new, progressive ideas had already taken root. During the reign of Elizabeth I (1558–1603) there was a building boom in country districts, because sheep-farming and the wool-trade were restricted and a 'back to the land' campaign instituted. At this time many Continental refugees settled in England,

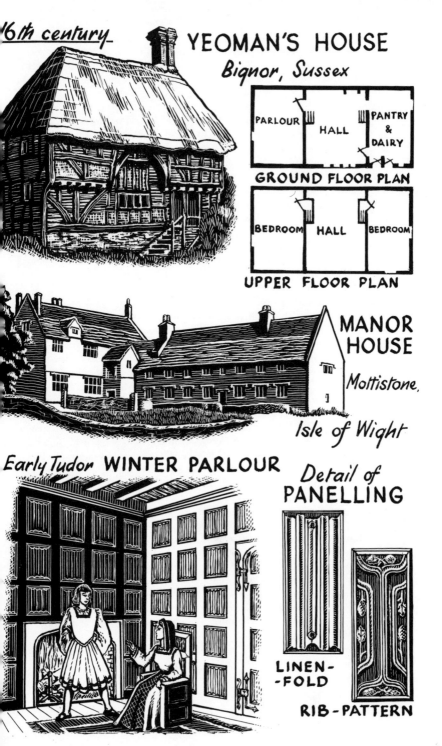

16th century

YEOMAN'S HOUSE
Bignor, Sussex

PARLOUR	HALL	PANTRY & DAIRY

GROUND FLOOR PLAN

BEDROOM	HALL	BEDROOM

UPPER FLOOR PLAN

MANOR HOUSE

Mottistone,

Isle of Wight

Early Tudor WINTER PARLOUR

Detail of PANELLING

LINEN-FOLD

RIB-PATTERN

27

large numbers of them being skilled craftsmen. Conversely, many Englishmen travelled abroad both on trade-missions and voyages of exploration. So spread the new ideas of the Renaissance, grafted, with the traditional British genius for adaptation and compromise, on to existing styles and methods.

What were these new ideas? Most evident was a passion for symmetry and balance in architecture, not always a feature of medieval planning which was more haphazard. This meant the sacrifice and replanning of the traditional, lofty hall which had often necessitated the placing of the main entrance at one end of the house. Tradition dies hard, and it will be seen from the plan of the yeoman's house (27), built during the reign of Henry VIII, that, even in such a comparatively humble dwelling, a lofty hall reaching from ground to roof was retained. Separate staircases to bedrooms were therefore necessary. The upper floor projected beyond the lower walls; this form of construction, involving massive horizontal beams, was called a *jetty*, a typical feature of the 15th and 16th centuries. These *jetties* acted as a counterbalance to ensure that the floor of the upper storey remained rigid and did not sag; it also gave some protection from the weather to the lower walls, often made of *wattle and daub*.

The stone-built manor house in the Isle of Wight (27) is early 16th-century, although it might appear to be more typical of the preceding period. It is a fact that, the farther country houses were from London and the home counties, the more 'old-fashioned' they tended to be. The windows are rectangular, not arched in medieval style (21); two or more areas of leaded panes of glass are divided by vertical stone 'bars' or *mullions*.

It was now more fashionable to cover interior walls with panelling than with tapestries (27). The comfortable *winter parlour* shows the overall effect. *Linenfold* panelling (27, 29) was very characteristic of this period; the *rib-pattern* design, based on conventional vine leaves and bunches of grapes, was also popular. When one considers that no mass-production methods existed, so that each panel was an individual piece of carving, the skill and patience of Tudor craftsmen can be appreciated. The horizontal beams spanning timber ceilings were sometimes elaborately carved.

The drawings on pages **29–37** illustrate some of the varied styles of domestic architecture seen side-by-side during the 16th century. The tile-hung house (**29**) was so called because the exterior walls of the upper storey were covered with roof-tiles, the lower walls being built of brick. As tiles were expensive, this style could be adopted only by those who could afford it and was not therefore as common as other types of construction. The upper floor was *jettied*.

The *cruck* houses (**29**), still constructed in the Saxon method (**13**), show that tradition persisted after more than 600 years. Note that they were built on a brick foundation.

Similarly, the ground-floor walls of the Suffolk farmhouse (**29**) were of stone, the two upper floors being timber-framed.

TILE-HUNG HOUSE *Surrey*

CRUCK HOUSES *Gloucestershire*

FARMHOUSE *Suffolk*

LINENFOLD PANEL

29

Page **31** illustrates one of the oldest surviving houses on the Channel Island of Guernsey. It is not particularly typical of the various styles of Tudor architecture popular on the mainland, but is remarkable for its curved buttresses, built of local granite in blocks of assorted sizes and shapes. These are also of different colours, tawny, pink and blue-grey. This shows how local resources have produced regional characteristics in building, for example Cotswold stone, and the plentifully wooded country of south-east England. Without modern drainpipes and windows, this house probably looked much the same in the 16th century as it does today.

The town house in Tewkesbury, with its ground floor walls built of brick and its three upper floors all *jettied*, shows that in 16th-century towns, as in 15th century city streets (**25**), builders were anxious to utilize all available space. Then, as now, if they could not extend their houses sideways, they stretched upwards. The topmost gables jutted crazily outwards and mullioned windows projected.

The Norfolk cottage, also shown opposite, was originally erected in the early 16th century, although it is thought that the deep band of decorated plasterwork and the rectangular window-panes were added at a later date.

ELIZABETHAN MANOR HOUSE

Berthelot Street,
St. Peter Port, Guernsey
c. 1550

Tewkesbury

Norfolk

On page **33** is shown the Market House at Midhurst. It is stated by the County Archivist that a plot of land, on which the Market House had been newly built, was granted in 1552 by Sir Anthony Browne to the burgesses. In 1945 the author painted a watercolour of this house; the half-timbering, usually of oak, had been allowed to weather to a delightful shade of greenish-grey, which looks far more harmonious than startlingly darkened beams against white or cream plaster. The brickwork on the side of the house shown in shadow provides a clue in determining its date. It is designed in an intricate herringbone pattern between half-timbering. Brickwork was brought to a fine art by Tudor craftsmen; a famous example of this may be seen at Hampton Court Palace.

On the left of the illustration is shown part of an adjacent building, the Spread Eagle Hotel, the earliest parts of which date from 1430.

Tudor furniture (**33**) was usually of solid oak, the design and carving becoming more ornate as the century progressed. Stools were often used, particularly as ladies' skirts became more and more voluminous; by the time that wide *farthingales* were worn during the reign of Elizabeth I, chairs had of necessity to be made without arms, to accommodate this cumbersome fashion.

Four-poster beds became massive and ornately carved. They could be completely enclosed by the overhead *tester* and curtains at the three open sides.

The fireplace illustrated shows Italian influence; this is a fairly modest design, with embellished painted coats of arms in relief, and the family motto. In the homes of wealthy nobility some chimney-pieces were extremely ornate, being adorned with flamboyantly carved figures in high relief.

PLASTER CEILING · c. 1600

The Market House, Midhurst Sussex

Mid-16th century

FIREPLACE c.1571

TUDOR FURNITURE

33

On page **35** is illustrated a typical 16th-century street in a country town, existing in the present day. Without the modern embellishments of telephone wires and drainpipes, this is how it must have looked when these houses were first built.

The Elizabethan mansion shows the effect of Renaissance ideas; the high *Dutch gables*, stepped and curved, were similar in design to those on many old houses still to be seen in Holland and South Africa. There were balustrades along the eaves. Windows were *mullioned*, and there were also high *oriel* windows. In order to achieve a balanced, symmetrical design and also an increased number of upstairs rooms without a series of separate staircases, the height of the hall was reduced to one storey. Having ceased to be a communal eating and sleeping place, the hall was rapidly approaching the modern conception of an imposing entrance-room with its central front door and with separate dining-parlour and withdrawing-room opening from it. As shown in the second of the following plans, it could even be placed off-centre—a most revolutionary idea!

A feature of large Elizabethan mansions was the *long gallery*, a large elongated room occupying a great amount of the first floor, as shown in the third of the following plans. It was often used to display family portraits, and was certainly an ostentatious room for pleasure and relaxation, demonstrating the taste and wealth of country gentlemen. This was a notable departure from the merely functional aspect of rooms in medieval houses.

The introduction of the long gallery illustrates the increasing emphasis on elegance, comfort and gracious living when grim, defensive buildings were no longer necessary.

Another Renaissance idea was to surround beautiful houses with *herbers*, *garths* or formal gardens. The Tudors loved flowers and fragrant herbs, both indoors and out, and their estates abounded in parkland, groves, arbours, fountains, statuary, mazes (*see* Hampton Court Palace), ornamentally clipped bushes (topiary), yew hedges bordering straight paths, and beds of sweet-smelling lavender, rosemary, marjoram and thyme.

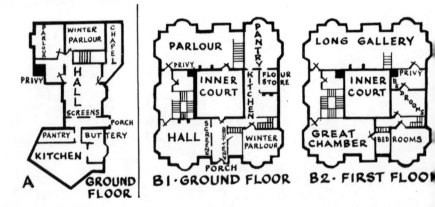

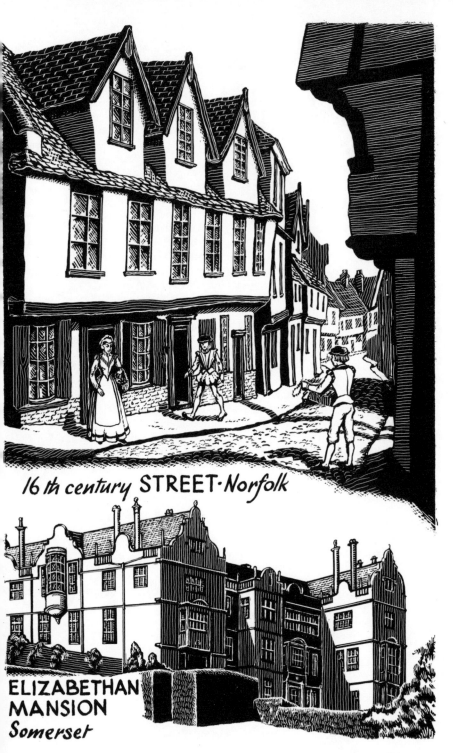

16th century STREET·Norfolk

ELIZABETHAN
MANSION
Somerset

ELIZABETHAN STAIRCASE

With the exception of rough ladders, medieval staircases were of stone, often within towers and therefore spiral. Finding these inconvenient, austere and reminiscently warlike, Tudor architects developed wooden staircases (**37**). Oak was customarily used and staircases progressed from plain erections to imposing and elaborately carved features of Elizabethan homes.

As panes of glass were now in general use, except in the poorest farm labourers' cottages, the design of leaded window-panes and glazing became increasingly fanciful during the 16th century (**37**). By the latter years of Elizabeth I's reign windows were often ornamented with painted coats of arms inset into small rectangular panes of glass.

Tall, decorative chimneys were a notable feature of Tudor architecture (**37**). They reached their highest peak of elaboration and intricate brickwork during the reign of Henry VIII (1509–47). It is a tribute to the skill of Tudor craftsmen that they were able to erect twisted, panelled and spirally-banded chimney-stacks. During the reign of Elizabeth I (1558–1603) the design of chimneys became simpler and less fantastic. In Elizabethan England, famous builders and architects were beginning to be known by name, for example John Abel, a great carpenter of Herefordshire, John Thorpe, whose architectural drawings still exist, and Richard Dale who, in 1559, constructed the splendid timbered bays of Moreton Old Hall in Cheshire (**37**). Here the *barge-boards* edging the gables were plain, but the modified *jetties* were decorated with plaster quatrefoils.

The great Inigo Jones was to follow; he was the first to introduce true Renaissance Classical architecture into England, during the early years of the next century.

LIGHTING

Soft wax or tallow candles in socketed candlesticks of brass, iron, latten (like brass), silver or gold. Chandeliers were hung by chains to overhead beams.

Pewter oil lamps with unplaited wicks were not satisfactory and were seldom used subsequently.

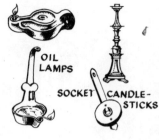

OIL LAMPS

SOCKET CANDLE-STICKS

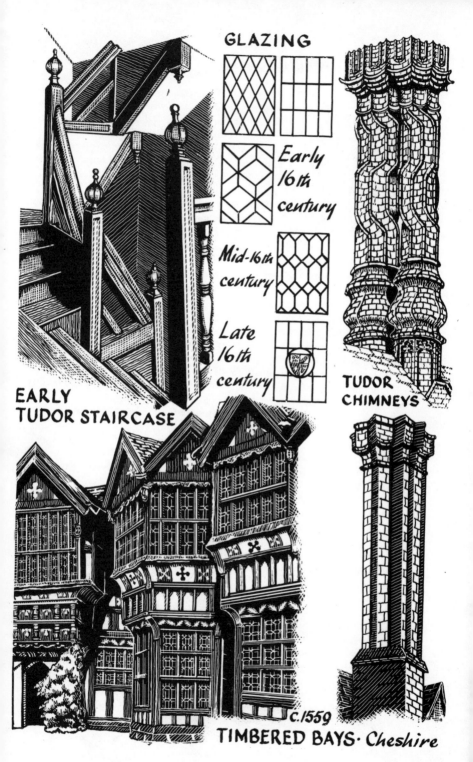

GLAZING

Early
16th
century

Mid-16th
century

Late
16th
century

TUDOR
CHIMNEYS

EARLY
TUDOR STAIRCASE

c.1559
TIMBERED BAYS · Cheshire

7 The Seventeenth Century

DOVECOTE·1632

THROUGHOUT THIS PERIOD, Renaissance ideas continued to be developed, and reached their climax in the architectural glories of Inigo Jones, Sir John Vanbrugh and Sir Christopher Wren. As these architects were mainly concerned with churches, palaces and public buildings, a detailed appraisal of their work is not within the scope of this book.

Various periods of design were named after successive monarchs: Jacobean, of the reign of James I (1603–25), Carolean or Caroline, relating to Charles I (1625–49), and Charles II (1660–85), Queen Anne (1702–14), William and Mary (1689–1702).

National events affected architecture: the Puritan régime of the Commonwealth (1649–60) at best had a sobering and restraining effect on some aspects of house-design, sweeping away much badly executed and over-elaborate ornament, clearing the way for future achievements. At worst its joyless and fanatically repressive ideas led to desecration and vandalism.

Inigo Jones had enjoyed the royal patronage of James I and Charles I, becoming Surveyor General in 1615. He must have been most unhappy at the drab patronage and hostility of the dour Commonwealth officials, at whose hands he suffered financially for his Royalist sympathies and loyalty; he died in 1652 at Somerset House.

With the Restoration in 1660, ornament and exuberant architectural beauty were a natural expression of national joy.

Another event which affected house-building was the Great Fire of London in 1666. Large towns, and especially the City of London, were already congested. In 1583 Elizabeth I had attempted to restrict the density of population by ordering that no house be built unless it had at least four acres of land attached—a good idea for the country, even though builders evaded regulations by secretly prefabricating frames of timber houses and hastily erecting them on site; houses were thus built and occupied before a competent authority could enforce the law. But the rule was much too late and impracticable to apply to crowded cities. Lofty 15th- and 16th-century timbered houses were packed together. James I, unable to cope with the problem of overcrowding, was conscious of the fire-hazard and passed laws against building timber houses with overhanging jetties in towns; all new building must be of brick, and he said with pride, 'We had found our Citie and suburbs of London of stickes, and left them of brick', which was not wholly true. Jutting gables and overhanging *jetties* created not only a fire-hazard, but extremely insanitary conditions, slops and refuse being tossed out of windows into the street below, increasing disgusting smells and dirt, and no doubt enabling the Great Plague of 1665 to spread with thoroughness and deadly speed. It is said that these *jetties* saved many a passer-by from filthy drenchings. The Great Fire destroyed some 13,200 houses and devastated an area of 443 acres; streets were

CRUCK HOUSES

Gloucestershire

Herefordshire

FARMHOUSE
Surrey

GABLES

1624

MANOR HOUSE   Wiltshire

39

replanned and neat brick and stone houses rose from the charred ruins of the old wood-and-plaster City.

Another aggravating factor was a foretaste of our 19th- and 20th-century problems of overcrowded slums. For various reasons impoverished owners of large, dilapidated Tudor mansions had been forced to abandon their houses; some of these were appropriated by an incredible number of desperately poor families and became squalid tenements.

The pictures on pages **39, 41** and **47** show various types of farmhouses and country cottages. These have survived to the present day because they were of the better and more durable sort; owing to the extremes of wealth and poverty created by the wool trade in Tudor times, the poorest country folk still lived in flimsy, primitive hovels, often as squatters in roadside shacks. Old cottages still followed the Saxon and medieval pattern of a lofty hall with a smoky central hearth, but those that survived were adapted to normal two-storey dwellings by the insertion of a chimney-stack.

The *cruck* houses illustrated on page **39** show that the Saxon principle of construction (**13, 29**) still continued, whilst the Surrey farmhouse shows that the Renaissance passion for symmetry had not engulfed all building in country districts, although there were cases of pretentious fronts quite out of place on little houses. Large, formal manors were symmetrical, as shown by those in Wiltshire (**39**) and Dorset (**41**).

Ornamental gables (**39, 41**) continued to show Dutch and Flemish influence. They were of intricate brickwork or faced with stone, and were particularly popular in East Anglian towns.

From the Dorset manor houses of 1622 (**41**) it will be seen that tall, plain chimneys were grouped neatly and symmetrically; windows were still *mullioned*.

Country cottages were built in a variety of materials, depending largely upon local resources. Bricks were extensively used, as was Cotswold stone in Gloucestershire. Half-timbering and plaster were popular in well-wooded districts, and are a familiar sight in Warwickshire and Worcestershire. The quaint and picturesque *cob and thatch* cottages in Devonshire have become a modern tourist attraction. *Cob* means a mixture of clay, gravel and straw for building walls, similar to the ancient *wattle and daub*.

The stone Cotswold cottage is sturdy in construction and simple in design, owing nothing to sophisticated Continental influences. Indeed, Costwold builders and craftsmen developed their own simple style, featuring small *mullioned* windows and large stone roofing 'slates'.

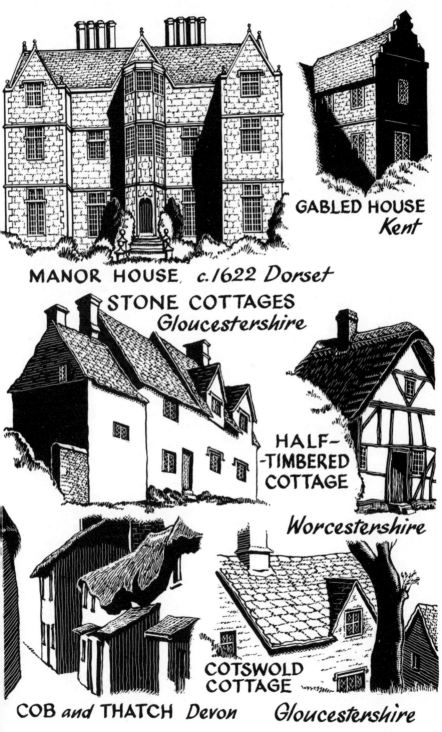

GABLED HOUSE
Kent

MANOR HOUSE, *c.1622 Dorset*

STONE COTTAGES
Gloucestershire

HALF-
-TIMBERED
COTTAGE

Worcestershire

COTSWOLD
COTTAGE

COB *and* THATCH *Devon*   *Gloucestershire*

The Queen's House at Greenwich (**43**) was built on land granted by James I to his wife Anne of Denmark. She commissioned Inigo Jones to design an elegant house to replace an old gatehouse and to enable her to cross dryshod the main Deptford-Woolwich highway. Building was begun in 1616, but ceased in 1618, a year before the Queen's death. It was not resumed until 1629, for Queen Henrietta Maria. In 1617 the project had been called a 'curious device' costing 'above £4,000'. It was, in effect, a bridge connecting the palace garden with Greenwich Park, designed in two blocks with a central room spanning the road; it became a sumptuous retreat for the Queen, where she could live in pseudo-simplicity. The design was Italian in style. After the Restoration the architect John Webb filled in the east and west elevations through which the road had passed, making the house a solid rectangle. The illustration shows the south front, the inclusion of classical columns resembling the Villa Mollini near Padua. Symmetrically planned rooms and staircases, moulded and painted plaster ceilings and a square salon with a marble floor were in the Italian style.

The house suffered many subsequent changes. In 1708 *mullioned* windows were replaced by deeper sash ones. In the early 19th century, no longer a queen's residence, it was divided into five tenements. Fortunately, damaged interior decoration was subsequently restored by the Ministry of Works. It had been spared from demolition when Greenwich Palace was rebuilt, this reprieve being due, it is said, to Queen Mary II's respect for the work of Inigo Jones. Thus survived his earliest masterpiece.

The *coved*, or concave, arched ceiling was one of the many popular styles of decorative plasterwork. Ornamental motifs included repeating geometrical patterns, floral, natural history and heraldic devices.

The type of doorway designed by Inigo Jones for the Palace of Whitehall was often seen in grand houses.

Sash windows, with rectangular panes, appeared after 1685. Elaborately carved four-poster beds were less massive than Elizabethan ones (**33**).

The *court cupboard* of 1610 has plainly panelled doors surmounted by a recessed shelf with carved *balusters* and *cornice*.

Bedding included 'a tester of arras and three large stained worke curtains, a large feather bed, a wolbed, a matt, twoe coverings of arras, a blanckett, a boulster and twoe pillows'. Bedroom furniture included chairs, stools, 'coffers' and 'cipres chestes' (to repel moths) and several 'chamberpotts'.

Chairs were of carved oak; upholstery was not generally introduced until after 1660. Cushions or cloth bags stuffed with wool had been used since late medieval times, hence the Lord Chancellor's 'woolsack' in the House of Lords.

Gate-leg tables, with hinged flaps, had appeared by 1645.

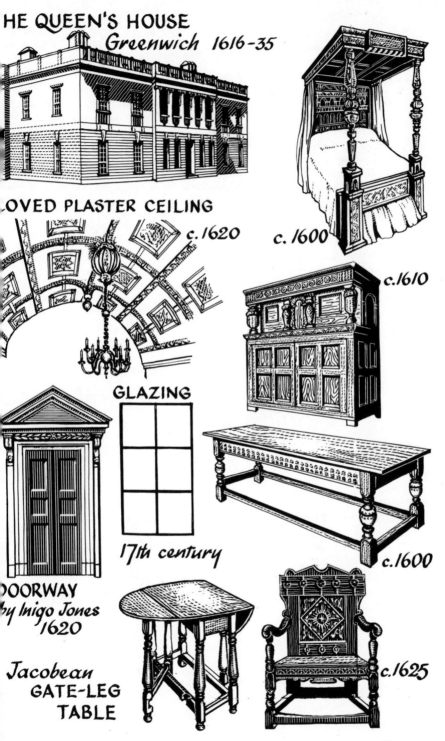

THE QUEEN'S HOUSE
Greenwich 1616-35

...OVED PLASTER CEILING

c. 1620

c. 1600

c. 1610

GLAZING

17th century

...OORWAY
*by Inigo Jones
1620*

c. 1600

Jacobean
**GATE-LEG
TABLE**

c. 1625

43

The Oxfordshire mansion, Burford Priory, built by Speaker Lenthall, is a further example of Renaissance symmetry, the central entrance being made important by carving and *pilasters*.

The plan of the mansion illustrated (**45**) is not of Burford Priory, but of a large house typical of the period. The hall was reduced to modern proportions, the staircase was imposing and the grand salon usually overlooked the garden and extensive parkland. A library was an innovation, sometimes decorated in mock-medieval fashion, in order to impart an atmosphere of scholarly research. High bookcases lined the walls.

Royalist and Puritan styles of decoration are contrasted.

The Royalist hall of 1641 has plastered walls, classical Ionic columns, a moulded ceiling in high relief, moulded *pediments* above doorways and a chequered marble floor in the Italian mode, rather more suited to the Italian climate than to English winters.

The Puritan room is plainly panelled in wood and the flat ceiling crossed by beams.

The ground-floor plan of a one-parlour cottage with two rooms above, is typical of many East Anglian cottages based on Flemish ideas. A central chimney-stack served back-to-back fireplaces in kitchen and parlour; a tiny entrance lobby contained a spiral wooden staircase and gave separate access to both downstairs rooms. Wealthier householders might have a two-parlour cottage.

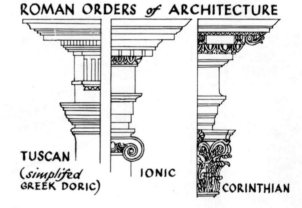

ROMAN ORDERS *of* ARCHITECTURE

TUSCAN
(*simplified*
GREEK DORIC)

IONIC

CORINTHIAN

GROUND FLOOR PLAN
of MANSION

DINING ROOM

PANTRY

KITCHEN

HALL

PRIVY

PRIVY

SALON

DRAWING ROOM

LIBRARY

ROYALIST HALL
c.1641

Oxfordshire   c.1640

PURITAN PARLOUR
c.1645

GROUND FLOOR
PLAN of COUNTRY COTTAGE

PANTRY

KITCHEN

FIRE-PLACES

PARLOUR

45

The Berkshire mansion Coleshill House (**47**) was the work of Sir Roger Pratt, an architect in association with Inigo Jones, and was completed in 1664. The design of the roof was *hipped*, meaning that, dispensing with traditional gables, the pitch of the four sides was curved slightly upwards at the eaves. Light for the top floor was provided by *dormer* windows. The chimneys were large in proportion to the structure. Shutters protecting ground floor windows were a Continental fashion, necessary as a shield from hot sunshine in warmer climates than that of Britain.

The Gloucestershire manor house also has a hipped roof and dormer windows.

The following selection of farmhouses and country cottages in a variety of styles and materials, shows that, except in cases where pretentiousness overcame simplicity, utility rather than formal symmetry still dominated building in rural areas. The Herefordshire house and the interior of a Kentish farmhouse illustrate that beams and half-timbering were used both as structural items and decoration inside and out.

The Sussex house is *tile-hung*, a costly style occasionally seen in Tudor times (**29**). Tiles were usually bedded in mortar to ensure water-tight protection and were either plain roofing tiles, or with decorative lower sides known as 'fish-tailed' or 'imbricated'.

The Essex and Kent farmhouses are *weather-boarded* in oak or elm boards 6–7 inches wide, overlapping for 1–1½ inches. Oak and elm were found to weather well, but if not thoroughly seasoned, had a tendency to warp and lift their nails. Baltic pine wood was imported and it was written in 1641 that 'firre deals are accounted better for bordenynge than oake that hath not had time for seasoninge'. Both these farmhouses have large chimneys.

The little Cambridgeshire cottage was similar in layout to the one-parlour cottage shown on page **45**.

LIGHTING

Soft wax or tallow candles in candlesticks, candelabra or chandeliers. As wicks were unplaited and the soft wax dripped easily and unevenly, frequent snuffing was necessary.

**CHANDELIER,
CANDLESTICKS &
SNUFFER**

Berkshire 1664

Gloucestershire

Herefordshire

Kent

Sussex

FARMHOUSE
INTERIOR

Essex

Cambridgeshire

Kent

47

BRACKET CLOCK

1660

The illustrations on pages **49** and **51** are of houses, fittings, decoration and furniture of the Restoration period and last years of the century.

The staircase of 1662 was designed by John Webb. The turned *balusters* appear less massive than the staircase of 1664, which has elaborately carved panels of acanthus leaves, a Dutch fashion popular for only about 20 years. The *newel posts* were treated as pedestals supporting carved urns of fruit and leaves. This is in Eltham Lodge, Kent, the exterior of which is shown opposite. It was built of brick with stone classical columns flanking the front door.

The Essex street of 1675 shows that the eastern counties favoured a transitional Renaissance fashion called *pargeting* or decorative plasterwork. The word is derived from the old French *parjeter* (to cast over a surface) or from the Latin *spargere* (to spread or sprinkle). The spaces between the constructional timbers were first filled with plaster; when this had dried, plaster, toughened by binding with hair or cow-dung, was spread over the whole surface including timbers, and then decorated in simple panels with a 'comb' or elaborate designs. Medieval plasterers had been known as *pargeters*, but in the 17th century the term meant exterior wall decoration, comprising moulded panels, festoons of fruit or flowers, or human and animal figures in high relief.

Classical *pediments* on porches and both exterior and interior doorways were extremely fashionable.

The Hertfordshire house (**51**) shows the *Palladian* style of architecture named after the Italian architect Andrea Palladio. Inigo Jones had travelled in Italy and had carefully studied this style, which featured Classical columns (**44**). While this pseudo-Classical style could be most imposing and beautiful when designed by a master who understood proportion and balance, less discerning and less capable imitators sometimes let their passion for Classical details run amok in works of tasteless over-elaboration.

The Sussex house (**51**) is of the William and Mary period. The roof was more steeply pitched than in previous years. It bears the date of its construction on the *soffit* of the hood over the front door. Typical of this date were the panelled brick chimneys; the windows were *wood-mullioned*, not sash. Although these had already been introduced, like all structural innovations they were first embodied in grand houses and only gradually in less pretentious ones.

Examples of William and Mary houses, including a charming one of 1694, duly recorded over the front door, may be seen in Hampstead Village, London.

The Yorkshire farmhouse near Otley (**51**) is a sturdy, stone-built structure roofed with heavy 'slates' of locally-quarried stone. These were fixed with oak pegs to oak laths, the joints being weather-proofed with moss. The topmost roof-ridges were of stone, lead being seldom used.

RESTORATION

1662

1664

Kent 1663

Essex 1675

PARGETING
1680

PORCHES

WALNUT CABINET

Interior walls of houses were often of coloured plaster, with panels left for mural paintings, sometimes of exotic and fantastic landscapes (**51**), or for the insertion of prized pictures.

Alternative wall-decorations were elaborately carved panels bearing clumps of flowers, foliage and cherubs' heads (**51**), or plain panels bearing swags or festoons of fruit and flowers. The carving of Grinling Gibbons was famous. First brought to the notice of Charles II in 1671, Gibbons later worked much under the patronage of Sir Christopher Wren. Some of his finest work may be seen in St. Paul's Cathedral.

The armchair shown features wickerwork, introduced after the Restoration, and an upholstered seat. The turned spiral legs are characteristic.

As William III came from Holland, Dutch furniture was fashionable, and the arts of veneering and marquetry were introduced. Grained walnut veneer was applied to a pine or beech foundation. Another new decorative process was gilt *gesso* (from the Italian word for plaster), used on tables and mirrors but too fragile for chairs. After 1660 lacquered cabinets on ornate gilt stands were fashionable, whether of genuinely oriental design imported by the Dutch East India Company, or manufactured in England or Holland.

Bed curtains were made of damask, satin, or velvet imported from Genoa. A late Stuart or William and Mary bed (**51**) was extremely tall, the cornice of the *tester* reaching the ceiling. The bedhead or *pillow-board*, and the cornice were of carved wood and could be further embellished with velvet or damask glued on. The *head valance*, edged with fringe or *galloon* (gilt braid), hung from the tester.

Many windows were bricked up because of the Window Tax of 1695.

Gentry were leaving crowded London; formerly palatial houses along the Strand became the notorious district 'Alsatia'. Owners planned 'conversions' to tenements and made money from renting them.

A new type of house appeared, no longer built for a specific owner, but for rent. Thus began standardization of design and the work of the speculative builder. One of the first of these was the Fourth Earl of Bedford, who developed Covent Garden in 1630. William Newton planned Lincoln's Inn Fields, Lord Southampton owned Bloomsbury Square, Lord St. Albans owned St. James's Square. The surnames of Sir Thomas Bond, Richard Frith, Sir Thomas Clarges and Colonel Panton are familiar London street names. Nicholas Barebones or Barbon built the Barbon type of single-fronted terraced houses in Bedford Row, Essex Street, Newport Square, Red Lion Square, Villiers and Buckingham Streets. Landlords built as many houses as possible on their land, and replanning after the Great Fire enabled them to design whole streets and squares.

LACQUER CABINET

PALLADIAN STYLE

Hertfordshire · Late 17th century

Sussex 1699

FARMHOUSE · *Yorkshire*

PANELLING 1696

Late 17th century

BED 1699

CARVED PANELLING

1680

by

Grinling Gibbons

8 The Eighteenth Century

THIS PERIOD is often called the 'Age of Elegance'; costume, furniture, interior decoration and architecture were indeed elegant. The flourishing state of the arts and the sophisticated wit of society were further reflections of the new Elegance. It was, however, a period less notable for personal cleanliness than for powerful perfumes and pomades, and elegant luxury was sharply contrasted with squalor, poverty, degradation and vice at the other end of the social scale.

Architectural styles are identified with the reigns of kings and queens, and the 18th century comprises the close of the William and Mary period (1702), Queen Anne (1702–14) and the Georgian era spanning the reigns of George I (1714–27), George II (1727–60), and George III (1760–1820), the last of which included the Regency style at the beginning of the 19th century (*see* Chapter 9).

Naturally, as time passes, more old houses survive. In London, notwithstanding the destruction of wars and the necessary growth of modern building, many 18th-century houses are still used for normal living, rather than as historical show-pieces.

National upheavals during the 17th century had, as described, disrupted the spread of Renaissance culture, and the Restoration in 1660 had revived a sense of joy and exuberance in many aspects of social and domestic life. These circumstances, added to the ravages of the Plague and the Great Fire of London, enabled the genius of architects like Sir Christopher Wren (1632–1723) and the more flamboyant Sir John Vanbrugh (1664–1726), who designed Blenheim Palace, to be recognized and flourish. Their work was the culmination of the English Renaissance; Wren continued and adapted Classical styles of architecture to his own beautifully balanced designs, which were more restrained than the *Baroque* fantasies of Vanbrugh. Wren had been appointed principal architect for the replanning and rebuilding of the whole of the City of London, including St. Paul's Cathedral and 51 parish churches, replacing those destroyed in the Great

GARDEN PAVILION
Vanbrugh

Fire. He had studied French architecture in 1665 and, a man of many talents, he was also a scientist and astronomer. Receiving the royal appointment of Surveyor General on 28th March, 1669, he held it until 1718.

The exteriors of typical town houses of the Queen Anne and early Georgian periods are illustrated on pages **53** and **55**. It will be seen that, except for Classical pillars and ornate, projecting porches, the façades of houses were quite flat, the effect being accentuated by the sash windows introduced at the end of the preceding century. There was usually a basement below ground-level.

LONDON HOUSES   c. 1700

Marlborough House, London   1709

Hampshire   c. 1715

Wiltshire
Early 18th century

53

Marlborough House, formerly the residence of Queen Mary, and now used for conferences of Government and Commonwealth statesmen, was designed by Wren or possibly his son, in 1709. The drawing (**53**) is based on an engraving of 1754.

The Hampshire house of 1715 (**53**) was designed for his own use by a leading Baroque architect named Thomas Archer, Groom Porter to Queen Anne, George I and George II, and architect to the Duke of Devonshire at Chatsworth.

The Wiltshire house (**53**) is considered to be the work of a local craftsman following the style of Vanbrugh, though in a restrained mood. It shows an interesting feature arising from national events of the time; there are several blank, bricked-up windows. These may have been originally and deliberately designed as such, in mute protest against the detested Window Tax imposed in 1695, or subsequently blocked up to reduce the levy.

The Cambridgeshire house (**55**), built in Wisbech about 1722, has a restrained and symmetrical façade, giving little indication of the elaborate panelling, carving and plaster-work of its interior.

The Kent house, built about 1725, is thought to be the work of Thomas Archer.

The Hampshire house of 1727 was built by John James for his own use. His architectural work, often featuring brick embellished with stone columns, was influenced by Wren and Vanbrugh. The placing of the numerous chimneys continues the Renaissance desire for orderly symmetry. James was also an accomplished planner of formal gardens, paying particular attention to the effective use of water and of vistas through plantations.

The Bristol house, built in 1730, is well-proportioned, with dormer windows above the parapet. Its decoration is restrained, the keystones above each window being carved to represent human faces, and the front door being surmounted by a semicircular or *segmental* hood.

Doorways and porches were elaborately carved at this time and usually embodied Classical columns. Doors, both interior and exterior, were, from about 1720 onwards, generally of mahogany, the popularity of which replaced that of oak, deal and pine. In order to give light to the staircase, especially of terraced houses, glazed *fan-lights* were installed above front doors, so called because the design was often based on the radiating slats of an open fan. *Pediments* were either rectangular, *segmental* or triangular.

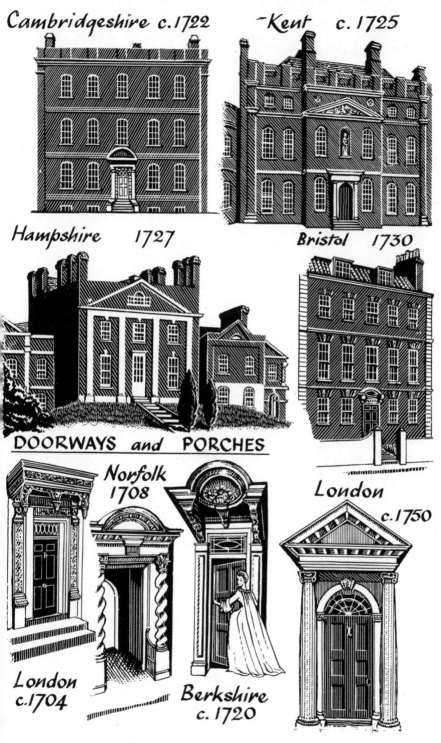

Cambridgeshire c.1722

Kent c.1725

Hampshire 1727

Bristol 1730

DOORWAYS and PORCHES

Norfolk 1708

London c.1750

London c.1704

Berkshire c.1720

55

Except for ornate and projecting porticos, the overall façade of an early 18th-century street (**57**) was flat and fairly even, as opposed to the jutting gables and *jetties* of medieval and Tudor times.

An architectural style which developed during this period was *Baroque*. This term is sometimes used in a disparaging sense, to denote over-elaborate and often fantastic detail. Based on Classical ornament, it took liberties with the Classical orders of architecture, substituting adventurous exuberance for their restrained serenity. However, the English Baroque style never approached the wild flights of fancy of that seen in Italy, Austria and Germany. The decoration of the Somerset house built in 1735 shows Baroque influence.

Having considered a few London and provincial town houses, it is a contrast to take a look at small houses in the countryside. As shown by the ground-floor plan of a typical Georgian cottage, the layout was simple, and the upper floor usually consisted of two rooms.

Brick and *weather-boarding* were commonly used in the country. In the case of the first Kent house illustrated, bricks were decoratively arranged in a chequered design. Brick was probably the most extensively used building material during the Georgian period, although snobbish opinion favoured covering humble bricks with a layer of *stucco* to simulate stone,

SPINNING WHEEL

during the late years of the century. However, *cob and thatch*, timber-framed and stone cottages were still being constructed from local resources.

The living conditions of agricultural labourers were gradually becoming better, as many squires and landowners were building decent cottages for them. A prosperous yeoman farmer would wish to be up-to-date and sometimes embellished his small house with a stylish brick façade (**57**), maybe a little pretentious.

The semi-detached cottages built near Guildford are strangely modern in appearance, and were forerunners of much house-design common in the present day.

Early 18th century STREET
Bristol

Somerset 1735

BRICK and WEATHERBOARDED
HOUSES · Kent
Early 18th century

FARMHOUSE with Georgian
façade
Suffolk

SEMI-DETACHED
COTTAGES
Surrey

GROUND FLOOR PLAN of
Georgian COTTAGE

BACK KITCHEN & PANTRY

CHIMNEY
KITCHEN

CHIMNEY
PARLOUR

The exterior appearance of Georgian houses has now been considered; some interior fitments and furniture are illustrated on pages **59–65**.

Many valuable details of houses being built about 1700 and of their decoration and contents, were described by Celia Fiennes in her journal published as *Rides Through England on a Side Saddle*.

Staircases, while still ornamental, became less massive than those of the Restoration period (**49**). Intricately designed wrought-iron balusters replaced carved wood, giving a lighter and more delicate effect. The staircase of 1770 was built on a spiral construction, reverting to a medieval principle discontinued in Tudor times.

Interior doorways were an important feature of decoration. The triangular *pediment* often designed by Inigo Jones during the 17th century (**43**) was still popular, though most surfaces were subsequently ornamented, and not left to Classical simplicity. The heavy *pediment* was gradually superseded by a lighter *cornice*, the example of 1780 being in the delicate style of the brothers Adam. Doors were usually of panelled mahogany.

Costume affected furniture, particularly chairs; the increasingly wide hooped skirts worn by fashionable ladies of the 18th century made narrow armchairs impossible, so that stools or *tabourets*, first introduced at the French Court, became popular, as were chairs without arms, mahogany being frequently used in their construction rather than oak (**59**).

A famous furniture designer and superb craftsman of the period was Thomas Chippendale. From 1758 to 1780 he was the most fashionable cabinet-maker and upholsterer. The *cabriole* legs of the chair illustrated are characteristic both of his own work and of an entire style, much copied.

Many beautiful examples of 18th-century furniture may be seen in the Victoria and Albert Museum in London and in other public and private collections. Famous designers and craftsmen of the period included William Kent, Robert Adam, George Hepplewhite and Thomas Sheraton.

LIGHTING

WALL LANTERN
1750

Candles were still the principal means of illumination, set in ornate chandeliers, candelabra and wall-brackets made of brass, silver, carved wood or *gesso* (a kind of plaster of Paris composed of whitening and size, applied to wood in moulding and patterns and then painted or gilded). Single candlesticks were usually made of brass, iron or pewter, particularly in country districts.

Candles required constant attendance with a snuffer, but the quality of the wax was now improved by a hardening process, and dripped less.

STAIRCASES

c.1706

c.1715

c.1740

c.1770

INTERIOR DOORWAYS

1760

CHIPPENDALE CHAIR

1725

1730
TABOURET

c.1760

1770

MAHOGANY CHAIR

1780

59

On page **61** is a representative selection of pieces of 18th-century furniture; it would, of course, require a vast catalogue to provide a complete survey.

The love seat, designed for flirtatious couples, was said to be 'too large for one and too small for two'. It has the fashionable *cabriole* legs.

The side-table, known to have been designed by William Kent, is typical of his liking for bold festoons, scrolls and gryphons' heads. Such tables were usually marble-topped with gilded supports.

The satinwood toilet-table is slender in construction, and is an example of fine cabinet-work in the Louis-Seize (Louis XVI of France) style, decorated in the Classical manner. Classical urns, figures and motifs became increasingly popular because of the archaeological discoveries of the remains of the Roman cities of Herculaneum (in 1719) and Pompeii (in 1748). Differences of opinion arose as to the relative merits of Greek and Roman architecture and ornament.

The nest of drawers, made of satinwood (a favourite material of Hepplewhite), is decorated with small motifs derived from cameos, among floral swags.

The wine-cooler was designed by Robert Adam, and is an example of his more elaborate pieces, as, in general, his style inclined to severity and restraint as opposed to florid exuberance. With a matching sideboard, the wine-cooler is made of rosewood with metal decoration.

The mirror, designed by William Kent, has an elaborate carved and gilded frame which is surmounted by the Prince of Wales' feathers. Kent often used this motif in honour of his friend and patron Frederick Prince of Wales.

It is contrasted with the Adam mirror illustrated; the gilt frame of which includes a Classical urn, and is another demonstration that the Adam style was usually lighter and more delicate than that of many of his predecessors and contemporaries.

Clock-making had made great advances in skill and ingenuity. The elephant clock was a very fashionable item on a mantelpiece. The timepiece formed the howdah of an elephant, as in this example, or it might be mounted on a rhinoceros. The Chinaman on top of the clock is part of the modish Chinese and Oriental style called *Chinoiserie*. There were wallpapers, Soho tapestries, porcelain and lacquer cabinets, all featuring Chinese figures and motifs.

Long-case or grandfather clocks became popular not only in town and country houses of wealthy folk, but in humbler farmhouses. In the country, simple copies of fashionable designs were made by local clockmakers and carpenters.

LOVE SEAT
c. 1730

SIDE~TABLE
c. 1740

WINE-COOLER
(Designed by Adam)

SATINWOOD TOILET-TABLE

SATINWOOD
NEST of
DRAWERS

GRANDFATHER
CLOCK

MIRRORS

ELEPHANT CLOCK

(Kent)   (Adam)

61

Chimney-pieces (**63**) continued to be the dominant ornamental feature of fine rooms. They were designed to display carvings of Classical subjects, in high relief, beneath decorated, triangular pediments, or paintings inset below elaborate *cornices* (in the late Georgian period mirrors were inset below simpler *cornices* in the Adam style). The chimney-piece of 1728 is considered to show characteristics of Vanbrugh, although he had died two years previously. That of 1782, in the style of Robert Adam, was installed in an American house in Salem, Massachusetts.

The slight simplification from the massive chimney-pieces of Elizabethan and Jacobean times made the definite division of the mantel or fireplace and the overmantel covering the area of wall above the fireplace, more apparent. The mantel-shelf became a more prominent feature.

As the fireplace continued to retain its central importance, much thought and craftsmanship were expended on efficiently burning grates. Wrought iron *basket-grates* were manufactured, and sets of matching *fire-dogs*, tongs and shovels adorned marble hearths or *foot paces*.

In kitchens, open fires were still used, although baking ovens were increasingly used in private houses. Most household cooking was done on spits, and in cauldrons suspended on chains over open fires.

More chairs are illustrated opposite: a mahogany dining chair of 1730, with cabriole legs, and two light, upholstered chairs from a drawing-room and boudoir respectively. The two latter examples have gilded *gesso* frames. The settee of 1766 is taken from a painting by Zoffany, and has eight legs.

SANITATION

Having described domestic fires and cooking facilities, consideration of other public utilities, such as sanitation and water-supply, is appropriate. Drains were still rare; street gutters or *kennels* and any nearby river were still the repository for slops and rubbish, although the collection of slops had begun; they were carted away by night to pits outside cities and towns. It is a fact, however, that in matters of sanitation and plumbing, 18th-century cities were still inferior to a well-ordered Roman-British province of over 1,300 years before. Communal wells and pumps were used, and in new houses in parts of London, water from the River Thames was laboriously pumped through small-bore wooden pipes. The Chelsea Water Company was operating by 1721, and the Lambeth Waterworks by 1783. In cities near rivers, drinking water was sold in the streets by water-carriers bearing wooden barrels from shoulder yokes.

There were no baths in private houses, but a few communal bathing establishments were inaugurated and advertised.

In 1775 the first valve water-closet was patented by Alexander Cummings, and by the end of the century a few of these new-fangled appliances were being installed in town and country houses. They were connected to cesspools, sealed, deeply buried and cleared periodically. One cesspool served two or more houses or even a terrace.

Before condemning such methods as primitive, let us not forget that there are still dwellings without baths, and cottages in remote country

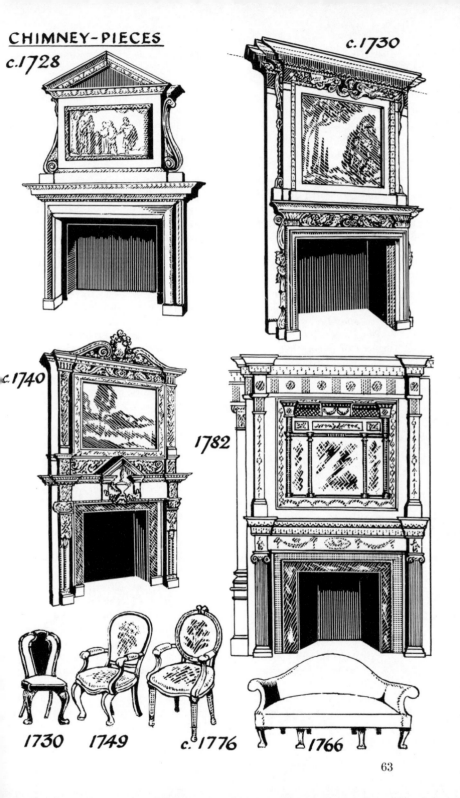

CHIMNEY-PIECES

c.1728

c.1730

c.1740

1782

1730   1749   c.1776   1766

63

districts without main drainage, where water has still to be fetched from wells or pumps!

Beds, massive and ornate, were most important articles of furniture. Four-poster beds were still in general use. The late Georgian bed shown opposite is a State Bed designed by Robert Adam about 1776.

The next model, formerly at Badminton and subsequently in the Victoria and Albert Museum, is a further example of the *Chinoiserie* mode, and may have been made in the Chippendale workshop. It is ornamented with gilded decoration on black lacquer, and surmounted by four dragons, the canopy being edged with gilt 'icicles'.

The tent bed was lighter in construction and far cheaper than ornate four-posters; it was therefore found in less-wealthy houses. Curtains were draped over a light iron framework trimmed with small brass *finials* at the top. As this type of bed was still used in the early 19th century, it is possible that its functional framework was the origin of Victorian brass bedsteads with plenty of knobs on them. A servant is shown in the illustration warming the bed with a copper warming-pan. Many of these are now kept as antique ornaments, but in the 18th century they were filled with glowing charcoal or cinders, and satisfied a very real need.

Details of typical ceilings of the period are also shown. There was a wide variety of decoration, including moulded plaster, flat or coved with or without inset-painted motifs circular or oval in shape, or, in great houses and public buildings, the whole ceiling might be painted, perhaps by Sir James Thornhill, Verrio or Laguerre. Ceilings designed by Robert Adam were often a large flat surface covered with plaster moulding in low relief, giving a simpler, lighter and more spacious effect.

WALL DECORATION

Where wooden panelling, either in its natural colour and wax-polished, or painted or stained, was sometimes used in the early 18th century, its overall effect could be sombre; painted plaster walls with mouldings ranging from the elegantly simple to the heavily ornate were frequently seen. Decoration less costly than painted frescoes was sought. As early as the beginning of the 17th century, *flock* wallpapers had been produced in France, and gradually came into use in this country. The method of production was to draw or stencil a repeating pattern on paper with an adhesive substance such as varnish or glue, then to scatter the surface with wool clippings which adhered to the sticky pattern and were removed from the remainder. Samuel Pepys had called it 'counterfeit damask'. Methods were improved during the 18th century and patterns were printed from wooden blocks. With the craze for *Chinoiserie*, brilliantly coloured Chinese papers were imported; as they were expensive and therefore restricted in availability, the manufacture of home-produced imitations was started, and flourished. Craftsmen and designers, including one John Baptist Jackson, broke away from Oriental subjects and produced wallpapers covered with pastoral scenes and romantic landscapes amid floral garlands. Jackson also decorated plain walls with prints and engravings framed in narrow strips of decorated paper.

BEDS *Late Georgian*

CHINOISERIE

TENT BED

CEILINGS

1760

1771 (Adam)   COVED CEILING *1777*

Returning to the exterior appearance of mid-Georgian and late Georgian houses (**67**), one can see from the Warwickshire house opposite that, while stone Classical columns extend to the total height of the building in the *Palladian* mode, the general effect is not over-elaborate, and the *architraves* of the central windows are simple in design. The façade of ordinary terraced houses remained flat and symmetrical.

The Chelsea houses combine two front doors under one triangular pediment. This was not a particularly happy design, as balance and proportion were upset.

The façade of the late Georgian terrace in Middlesex is varied by projecting bay windows with balconies. Georgian styles had a marked effect on the architecture of old American houses. The Americans had adopted *weather-boarding* on timber-framed houses. Sir Christopher Wren's name is connected with buildings in Williamsburg, Virginia, and George Washington's home in Mount Vernon has panelling and chimney-pieces typical of English houses of the period. Old prints of exclusive Boston, Massachusetts, show Georgian terraces, very English in appearance.

There is a surprising number of 18th-century and early 19th-century terraced houses left in parts of London, Canonbury for example, many houses dating from about 1787.

The larger and more elaborate house in Leicestershire was built in the style of Robert Adam. It features a Classical *pediment*, urns and festoons, and a symmetrical façade.

The Georgian *areas* shown opposite illustrate a constructional feature typical of the 18th and 19th centuries. Access to the basement rooms was by means of steps which led down from the street and formed a tradesmen's entrance to the domestic regions. Nowadays, when so many old houses, originally built when an ample domestic staff was obtainable, are converted into numerous flats, the original areas form separate entrances to basement flats.

FLOORS

In simple houses floors were of oak boards; in richer houses *parquetage*, a French fashion of inlaid patterns of differently coloured woods, was laid, or a chequered design of white and coloured marble.

Warwickshire · Mid – 18th century

Georgian AREAS · London

Chelsea, London

Late Georgian TERRACE
Middlesex

London
1787

HOUSE in Adam style · Leicestershire

On page **69** sophisticated town houses are again contrasted with simple country cottages.

The tall late-Georgian houses were originally built in Park Lane, London. They featured balustrades at roof-level and the many covered, cast-iron balconies show an Oriental influence, part of the *Chinoiserie* cult. Details of one such balcony is also illustrated. Originally, the floors of projecting balconies were of iron rods or slats forming gratings, not a very good idea when slender, high heels were worn.

The London house of 1792 was designed by S. P. Cockerell. This house features large Venetian windows inset in a relieving arch.

The 'Model Village' of Milton Abbas, Dorset, was laid out in 1786, although the primary reason for this apparent care of tenants is said to have been that the local landowner demolished the original village in order to make room for his fine new mansion.

An *outshut* (see page **12**) is an extension to a main building in the form of a lean-to addition on one side. In the Georgian period it was customary for the pantry to be located at the rear of a cottage, the main roof covering all rooms, with a steeply pitched *catslide* over the pantry. This demonstrates that the construction of country cottages tended to be functional rather than slavishly obedient to symmetrical planning.

Throughout the 18th century, as architectural designs were circulated in builders' handbooks, no doubt as self-advertisement for architects, the latest ideas on taste and fashion were available to country builders, and planning tended to become standardized throughout Great Britain. Such published manuals included *A Sure Guide to Builders* (1726), *The British Carpenter* (1733), *The Young Builder's Rudiments* (1730–6), *The Builder's Compleat Assistant* (1738), *Rural Architecture* (1750), *The Architectural Remembrancer* (1751), and many more.

PIANO *1790*

Late Georgian · London

Detail of BALCONY

COTTAGES in a "model village" · Dorset 1786

London · 1792

COTTAGE with OUTSHUT · Surrey

69

9 The Nineteenth Century

A DOG TURNSPIT c.1800

THIS PERIOD includes a continuation of the graceful late Georgian styles evolved in the last years of the 18th century; then followed Regency fashions in architecture and decoration, coupled with the Romantic Movement which resulted in the erection of many fantastic buildings, a notable example of which is the Royal Pavilion at Brighton. The desire for romantic novelty led to pretentious, pseudo-Gothic or sham-Elizabethan houses, 'antique' features of which were not so much integral parts of the structural planning as ornamental details added for effect. While an estimation of taste is a personal matter, and generalization is always dangerous, Victorian styles tend to be condemned as over-elaborate, vulgar and tasteless; but the seeds of bad taste were sown early in the century, with a loss of classical balance, simplicity and grace.

A national event which had widespread effects on domestic architecture and standards of living was the Industrial Revolution, which had begun in the second half of the 18th century. Factories and mills grew numerous, surrounded by dreary and squalid acres of 'back-to-back' houses. Gone were the charming market squares. In new towns these were no longer necessary as their produce consisted of factory products disposed of wholesale. The spreading areas of industrial towns were not planned; they grew spontaneously.

Today we are still troubled by slums and the problems of clearing them. It is a significant fact that the majority of houses fit only for condemnation are a legacy from the first half of the 19th century, during the period of tremendous industrial expansion.

The first illustration on page **71** shows the façade of late-Georgian town houses at the turn of the century. The flat and symmetrical effect is accentuated by the absence of a projecting porch, the front doors being surmounted by a simple brick arch. The first-floor windows have small wrought-iron balconies; shutters are used for both utility and decoration. There is an *area* leading to basement rooms.

The two designs for farmhouses, executed in 1807, show the growing desire, even in the less sophisticated country-side, for ornamental and pretentious houses. Their thatched roofs and arched doorways, more suitable to churches, seem artificial and out of place. In the 18th century widespread enclosure of common land had taken place, with the result that home-grown corn and livestock were insufficient to feed an increasing population, and grain was imported. Many farm labourers drifted to the new industrial towns. Some working farmers experienced great hardship, but the 'gentleman-farmers' and wealthy industrialists began to settle in the country, treating farming more as a hobby than a livelihood.

Devonshire · 1798–1800

1807

"Design for an Ornamental Farmhouse"
"Farmhouse for a Bailiff"
1807

Small TOWN HOUSE
Buckinghamshire · 1805

FARMHOUSE
1815

VILLA · Essex · c.1810

Regency HOUSE · Hove

71

William Cobbett, in vehement protest against abuses and the hardship caused in rural areas by the soaring prices of English wheat when imports were stopped by the Napoleonic wars, wrote his *Rural Rides*. He made scathing comments on the pretentious rather than functional aspects of farmhouses: 'And, which was the worst of all, there was a *parlour*. Aye, and a *carpet* and *bell-pull* too! One end of the front of this once plain and substantial house had been moulded into a "parlour"; and there was the mahogany table, and the fine chairs, and the fine glass, and all as barefaced upstart as any stock-jobber in the kingdom can boast of. . . .' Artificial gentility was more gently derided by the novelist Jane Austen.

The Romantic Movement was carried to ridiculous lengths. A designer named John Claudius Loudon considered that various amendments could be made to existing farmyard buildings, e.g. to make them look 'Grecian' add *pilasters* and *pediments*, to achieve a 'Roman or Italian' effect fix halfround tiles on roofs; for 'Gothic' have steep roofs, and insert buttresses and pointed arches here and there; for 'Old English' have *barge-boards* and latticed windows; to make buildings look 'Swiss' place a continuous verandah all round them. It is no wonder then that Cobbett wrote bitterly: 'When the old farmhouses are down (and down they must come in time) what a miserable thing the country will be! Those that are now erected are mere painted shells, with a mistress within, who is stuck up in a place she calls a *parlour* . . . the house too neat for a dirty-shoed carter to be allowed to come into . . . a constant anxiety to make a *show*. . . .' Between 1800 and 1837 about 30 books of designs for farmhouses were published, as against only eight during the whole of Queen Victoria's reign of over 60 years, and nearly all these books were addressed or dedicated to 'noblemen and gentlemen' and 'persons of more refined taste and discernment'.

Strictly speaking, the Regency lasted from 1810 to 1820, during the madness of George III, but Regency styles cannot be confined within those dates; the extravagances and scandals of the Prince of Wales (later George IV) and his Court were notorious and had extensive repercussions.

All three examples of Regency-style dwellings illustrated on page 71 show a taste for circular buildings. In fact, the Essex villa of 1810 reminds one of a biscuit barrel!

Brighton, Hove and Bath are particularly associated with Regency architecture, and there are still Regency crescents and terraces left in London, especially in the Regent's Park neighbourhood. Regent Street was laid out at this time, and there is still much evidence of the work of John Nash.

The construction of the large bay window of the house at Hove is reminiscent of medieval and Tudor *jetties*.

Typical Regency crescents and a square are illustrated on page 73 and also two period shop-fronts, with living accommodation above them.

London · 1812
(John Nash)

London · 1820–30
(G. Basevi)

SHOP FRONTS
Bridport, Dorset · c.1800

York · c.1810

Hove · 1825

Tunbridge Wells · 1830

Further examples of Regency villas, built during the reign of George IV, are shown on page **75**. It will be noticed that Classical columns were still featured as in the Gloucestershire villa, and that the popular circular plan was not always followed; a compromise is shown by the large semi-circular bays of the Devonshire house of 1820.

The 'house in cottage style' built in the Isle of Wight is an excellent example of the 'cottage ornée' in the rustic style, for clients who yearned for the 'simple' life with comfortable rooms and plenty of servants, people who were laughed at by Jane Austen in *Sense and Sensibility*. The cottage was designed by Robert Lugar. Its steeply-pitched thatched roof was supported on rustic posts entwined with climbing plants. Said to be based on an enlarged and improved fisherman's hut, and built of local stone, it had six bedrooms and four reception rooms. As shown on the ground-floor plan, there were wide bay windows in the drawing room which had a fine view of the sea.

Typical chairs and a dining table of the period are shown on pages **75** and **77**. Favourite woods for construction were mahogany and rosewood.

"A Cottage Ornée adapted to receive Trained Foliages"

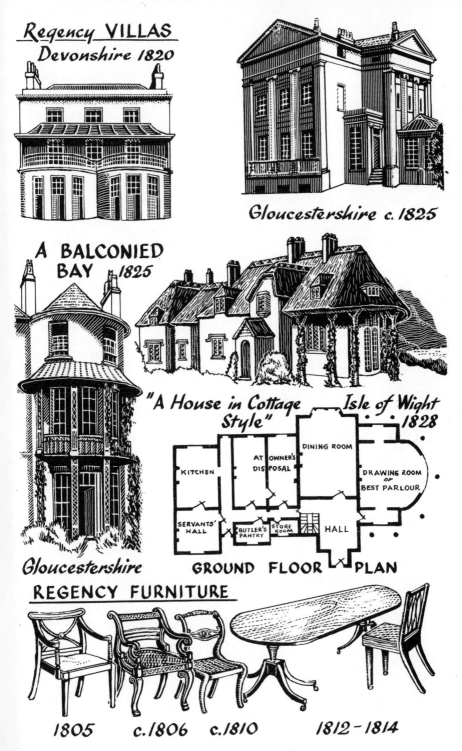

Regency VILLAS
Devonshire 1820

Gloucestershire c. 1825

A BALCONIED BAY 1825

Gloucestershire

"A House in Cottage Style"

GROUND FLOOR PLAN

- KITCHEN
- AT OWNER'S DISPOSAL
- DINING ROOM
- DRAWING ROOM or BEST PARLOUR
- SERVANTS' HALL
- BUTLER'S PANTRY
- STORE ROOM
- HALL

Isle of Wight 1828

REGENCY FURNITURE

1805   c.1806   c.1810   1812–1814

Information about typical articles of furniture in the early 19th century may be found in contemporary paintings and drawings of the period by such artists as Cruikshank.

The couch of 1806, with its scrolled head-rest, was used as a day-bed or *chaise-longue* by young ladies who, apparently, frequently suffered from 'declines' or attacks of 'the vapours'. This style of couch remained popular for many years, many Victorian versions of it being upholstered in horse-hair.

The chair of 1820 is an example of the 'cow-hocked' variety, in which the back legs are noticeably curved outwards, and incline together at the base. Beech wood, grained to look like rosewood, was extensively used.

Four-poster beds were still popular; the posts were fairly light in construction, and draperies were of light-weight material.

The Victorian period of design in architecture, furniture and draperies properly begins in 1837, when Queen Victoria ascended the throne. It should be remembered, however, that extravagancies of taste did not burst forth overnight, but were the outcome of tendencies established early in the century. With Victorian domestic architecture, however, it is less easy to associate the origins of any special style of architecture with the period as one can with Tudor, Jacobean and Georgian times. Victorian architects designed in revived Gothic, mock-Tudor, etc., and of these styles examples are shown in subsequent illustrations. There is something dubious in their adoption of the styles of previous centuries; in many instances the least desirable aspects of historic architectural styles have been copied without the functional grace of the originals.

The Lincolnshire house of 1837 was designed by Anthony Salvin. To conform to the contrived 'olde worlde' character of the house, leaded casements were installed, in lieu of sash windows.

However, not all early Victorian adaptations of historic architectural design were ugly. At a cursory glance, the façade of a row of houses in Canonbury would appear to be pure Georgian, in common with other terraces in the neighbourhood. Upon investigation it was established that the houses illustrated opposite were, in fact, built in 1845, and they look very charming.

The Kent house of 1841 was built at Ramsgate by A. W. N. Pugin for his own use. He was a fervent champion of the Gothic revival. He believed, with Ruskin, that architectural style was bound up with religion and morality. His conception of the Middle Ages was a kind of paradise, in which dedicated builders produced architectural glories for their love of God. The Renaissance and subsequent Reformation had, in his view, killed the Gothic purity of ideals.

Pugin assisted Barry in the design of the Houses of Parliament, begun in 1840.

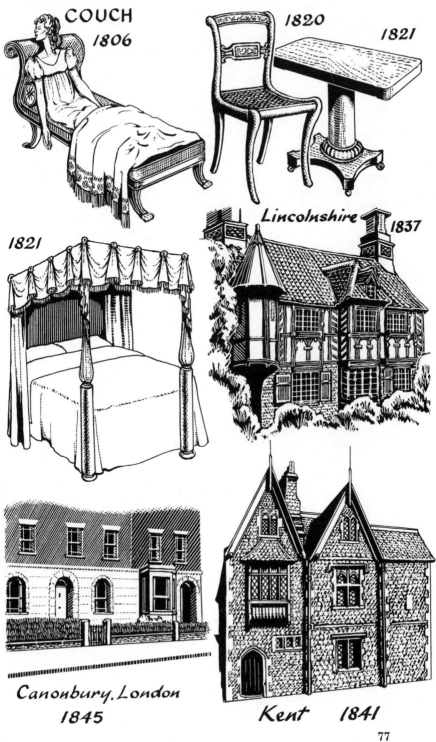

COUCH
1806

1820

1821

1821

Lincolnshire 1837

Canonbury, London
1845

Kent 1841

77

From the caption quoted below the Detached Villa in Kent, it will be appreciated that no effort was spared in emphasizing the desirability of embodying as many Gothic details as possible, such as decorated *barge-boards* on sharply pointed gables, half-timbering, massive chimneys and arched *mullioned* windows. This house was designed and illustrated in E. L. Blackburne's *Suburban and Rural Architecture*. Blackburne delighted, in a manner typical of the period, in picturesque erections in which Gothic, German, Italian, French, Swiss and somewhat vague 'Elizabeth' details ran riot. He prescribed, on all possible—and impossible—occasions, bands of bright red or yellow bricks and fancy roof tiles. Using the improved techniques of glass-manufacture, he could break away from small window-panes and substitute large plate-glass sash windows, which look most inappropriate when installed in determinedly 'antique' residences. He made great efforts to ensure that, in a row of houses, no two were identical, as he deplored the simplicity and repetitive detail of Georgian façades.

The papier-mâché bed of about 1850, to be seen in the Bethnal Green Museum, is an interesting example of a transitional half-tester style between a four-poster and a more modern style featuring only bedhead and foot-board. Papier-mâché means paper damped and pulped; it was then treated with sticky paste or size and moulded into a desired shape being painted and decorated with ornamental motifs sometimes with mother-of-pearl inlay on a black ground. It first became fashionable during the 1840s, and was used on many articles, ranging from tea-trays to beds and even piano cases. The draperies of the bed illustrated are green and gold.

In these days we are accustomed to exhibitions where a country's products are shown and publicized. In 1851, however, the Great Exhibition, housed in a splendid Crystal Palace originally erected in London's Hyde Park, was a unique event, demonstrating the latest mechanical marvels of the age, and Albert the Prince Consort was very much concerned with it. Some articles of furniture are illustrated opposite. These are based on contemporary illustrations in the catalogue of the Exhibition and are floridly typical. The chair was described as being 'constructed with the strictest attention to comfort'.

Papier-Mâché BED
c.1850

A Detached Villa in Kent, embodying "the principal characteristics of the English Gothic half-timbered house."

THE GREAT EXHIBITION · 1851

SIDEBOARD

CABINET

MODEL HOUSES *for the* LABOURING CLASSES

ALBERT COTTAGE
PIANOFORTE HARMONIUM

BOOKCASE

The sideboard of walnut with 'embellishments indicative of its use' was exhibited by Messrs. Hunter of London. It was massive in construction and seems of odd proportions, being strangely low and giving the impression of a settee rather than a sideboard. Vine branches twined round bacchanalian heads, and the legs were elaborately carved to represent cornucopia or horns of plenty, 'filled to overflowing with plentiful fruits of the earth giving large promise of abundance'. It was considered then to be 'altogether a well conceived production'.

The Prince Consort himself exhibited Model Houses for the Labouring Classes. The buildings contained four apartments (forerunners of our modern flats), each consisting of a sitting-room, kitchen, two small bedrooms, one large bedroom, a scullery and a decent water-closet. Buildings were fireproof and had their own water-supply. The total estimated cost of a block of four apartments was in the region of £450, and rents for each flat were 3s. 6d.–4s. per week.

A designer who had a tremendous influence on Victorian architecture, décor and furniture was William Morris (1834–96). His power lay not so much in his own revolutionary ideas, but in his association with a group of artists, designers and men of letters of the pre-Raphaelite school, which included Burne-Jones, Madox-Brown, Rossetti, Holman Hunt and the architect Philip Webb. It is said that Morris visited, as a youth, the Great Exhibition of 1851, and pronounced it all 'wonderfully ugly'. He was revolted by the ostentatious ornament, which was intended to call attention to its owner's wealth. At Oxford Morris was influenced profoundly by Ruskin's writings on Gothic architecture, and he himself wrote on the subject when he founded the Kelmscott Press many years later. He was very versatile, being an architect, painter, writer and poet. He also founded in 1861 the firm of Morris, Marshall, Faulkner & Co., with offices in Red Lion Square, London. The firm designed furniture, wallpaper, glass and fabrics.

In 1859 Philip Webb designed the Red House for William Morris. It was destined to become the prototype of many houses built later in garden cities. Its sensible, functional simplicity was a striking contrast to Victorian Gothic extravagances. The exterior and some interior features are illustrated opposite. The modern desire for a sunny southern aspect to the sitting-rooms was not considered, but the house of red brick was well planned, the kitchen and scullery being conveniently situated on the ground floor instead of in a dreary basement.

Although there were many Gothic details such as arched doors and windows, these features were not allowed to detract from comfortable living, practical sash windows being installed instead of mullioned ones. The exterior drawing shows the well outside the main door.

THE INFLUENCE of WILLIAM MORRIS

Red House, Bexley, Kent
1859 (Philip Webb)

FIREPLACE

CLOTHES PRESS
and HALL SEAT

STAIRCASE at Red House   SETTLE   DESK

81

The drawing of the staircase (81) shows also the use made of brick-work arches and beams. Although the Morris workshops produced many popular wallpapers embodying designs of fruit, flowers and birds, the walls of the Red House were either left plain or hung with various fabrics, on which were worked figures and floral designs in coloured wools, some by Morris himself, much to Rossetti's disapproval.

The brick fireplace (81) in the Red House dining-room was probably one of the earliest of its type. The wooden settle, designed by Philip Webb, was in startling contrast to typical heavy and ornate Victorian sofas. The com-bined clothes' press and hall settle was decorated by Rossetti. The desk, also designed by Webb, shows that current fashions in Victorian furniture were not at all suitable for the Red House.

A typical William Morris room is illustrated on page 83. Any fashion or school of thought, good in itself, is often carried to ridiculous extremes, and opponents of the simple style scathingly termed it 'greenery-yallery' because a favourite colour-scheme for interior decoration was a delicate pale green, which contrasted sharply with the prevailing crude and violent colours of Victorian décor. Aniline dyes had been invented by Perkin in 1856, and their harsh, bright colours in the early years of their use were an unpleasant alternative to the softer tints of the vegetable dyes previously used.

Many ladies devoted to the Morris style exchanged their voluminous crinolines for would-be romantic draperies, and, attempting perhaps to look like 'The Blessed Damozel' by Rossetti, drifted among their simple furniture and occupied themselves in 'arty-crafty' pursuits.

The 'Peacock' tapestry was designed by William Morris and produced by his firm. Composed of decorative bird and floral motifs, it was woven in soft shades of green, brown, pink, light blue and Prussian blue. The illus-tration beneath it shows the rose-and-lily damask designed by Morris. Another design was his 'Evenlode' chintz; on a green background was a repeating pattern of carnations amid conventional floral motifs.

Notwithstanding all its amenities, the Red House did not contain a bathroom. People who wanted an occasional bath, placed a hip-bath in front of a cosy fire, and servants brought cans of hot and cold water. The more progressive folk of about 1850 used the primitive contraptions illustrated opposite, two early forms of shower-baths.

With the growth of industrialism, more and more workers had dirty jobs. As they lived in wretched little back-to-back houses without decent sani-tary and bathing facilities, an Act of Parliament was passed in 1846 'to encourage the establishment of Public Baths and Wash-houses'. Fitted baths were still a luxury, and many houses were still built without them.

DINING ROOM

"Peacock" TAPESTRY

Rose & Lily DAMASK

BATHS

HIP BATH

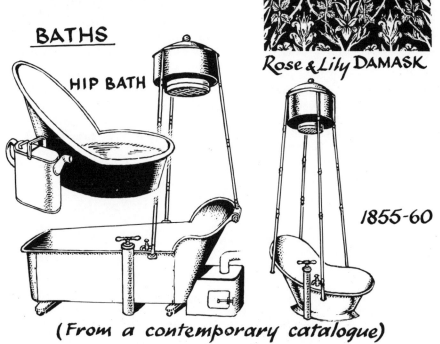

1855-60

(From a contemporary catalogue)

Except in rich folk's houses, the average dwelling was provided only with an outside privy in the backyard, often referred to as 'Jericho'. It was drained by a sunken cesspool, and this could be a dangerous practice when the supply of drinking water depended on sinking a well. The contamination of water led to outbreaks of cholera and fever. There were communal cesspools in Red Lion Square and Bedford Row, London, up to 1854. A sewer had been constructed in the Strand in 1802, which probably simply ran into the Thames or the River Fleet. But most people's houses were not near enough to be connected with the sewer. London was not provided with main drainage or a sewage system until 1865. But even this did not stop river-pollution.

Early main-water pipes were made of hollow elm-trunks. Lead water-cisterns had been invented during the 18th century, and in 1724 it had been made obligatory in London for roofs to be fitted with gutters and drain-pipes.

As a step towards making water-closets more common inside houses, inventors had tried since 1596 to make them less offensive by means of valves and traps. Scant attention was paid to adequate ventilation. While most contrivances were not entirely satisfactory, they paved the way for decent, modern sanitation.

As late as 1871, the Prince of Wales, later King Edward VII, contracted typhoid fever because of bad drainage in a Yorkshire house. Public attention was focused on the problem, and this brought about much improvement in drainage and plumbing by the end of the century.

The 'first-class' farmhouse illustrated opposite, determinedly 'Elizabethan' in style, but with a clumsy Gothic porch, shows that imitation of 'antique' styles was still rampant in 1861. While it contained a dining-room, drawing-room, nursery, numerous bedrooms and very adequate interior sanitary arrangements, there was still no bathroom. The house appears in Stephens' and Burn's *Book of Farm Buildings*.

The ornate porch of the 'rural' cottage in Berkshire, with its fretted *barge-boards*, does not seem to fit the simple building, but was probably its original owner's pride and joy. The house at Harrow, designed by R. Norman Shaw (1831–1912) has half-timbering, tile-hanging, pargeting, mullions—in fact, everything! Following in the footsteps of Philip Webb, Shaw gradually widened his scope beyond Gothic, through early and late Renaissance styles. He designed New Scotland Yard.

EFFECTS of INDUSTRIALISM

Back-to-back HOUSES

"Design for a first-class Farmhouse in the Elizabethan style" 1861

"Rural" COTTAGE · Berkshire

Harrow, Middlesex

The various houses illustrated on page **87** show Victorian architects' abiding preference for Gothic designs, plus Tudor barge-boards and 17th-century gables. Some enthusiasts had begun to realize however, that there was something false in attempting to recreate medieval architecture out of its true context, that is, away from the times and conditions in which the genius of the medieval masons flourished. When individual house-designs were left to the fancies of over-enthusiastic architects or owners, the façades of many city streets presented a regrettable, chaotic jumble of pseudo-historic features.

The house of 1877, designed by Philip Webb, and built at Smeaton, Yorkshire, illustrates the versatility of this architect. Departing from the ubiquitous Victorian Gothic, this house is in the style of the William and Mary period.

North Oxford houses of the period are brilliantly described by John Betjeman, the poet and authority on Victoriana, in his book *An Oxford University Chest*. The emphasis was on Gothic, and the houses there show the strong influence of ecclesiastic buildings and museums, and of the moral principles of Ruskin. Interior decoration featured stained glass and much varnished pitch-pine woodwork, similar to a clergy-house, and giving the impression of a high moral tone.

There was, however, much ugliness in execution. The pleasant colour and simplicity of stone often gave place to semi-glazed bricks of garish red, gloomy grey or sickly yellow, decorated with bands or arches of red or black brickwork. The houses in Kensington, London, were built about 1880 for artists. From left to right, their architects were J. J. Stevenson, William Burges and R. Norman Shaw respectively. The Stevenson house has high curved gables in 17th-century style.

LIGHTING

The planning of natural lighting for houses continued to be affected by the Window Tax which lingered until 1851. Rooms became increasingly cluttered with ornaments, dark panelling and heavy draperies, and the overall effect was gloomy and heavy.

As for artificial lighting, many improvements were made during the century. From about 1800-30, various types of oil lamps replaced candles. The flow of oil to wick was regulated by a clockwork pump, by a lever, or by piston and spring. Hanging lamps were used, which had a central container for oil, and three or more wick-holders protected by glass bowls, while any dripping oil was caught in a glass tray slung underneath. Table-lamps were also used.

Between 1830 and 1850 camphine lamps were invented; the light from them was satisfactory, but there was some risk of explosion. Until 1850, only animal and vegetable oils were available for illumination, but the discovery of mineral oil deposits enabled the petroleum lamp to be introduced.

VICTORIAN GOTHIC *Worcestershire*

c.1877 **Oxford**

1877 **Yorkshire**
(Philip Webb)

c.1880

London

87

Meanwhile, a revolutionary and labour-saving device was slowly becoming available in towns—gas. As early as 1805, several factories in Manchester had been lighted by this novel method. In 1807 successful experiments were made in street-lighting, first in Pall Mall, then in other parts of London, and its use was extended to the interior lighting of buildings. The use of this 'brilliant, steady and beautiful flame' became fairly general. During the 1890s electricity was introduced. Pall Mall was, in 1897, again selected for the experimental use of the 'new illuminant'.

A library of 1855 is illustrated on page **89**. It contains heavy furniture, unyieldingly upholstered in horsehair, massive bookcases and oil lamps.

During the second half of the 19th century, some of the most extreme effects were achieved in exterior and interior decoration. Maybe the placid domesticity of most women's lives led them to indulge in adventurous, over-elaborate ornament in their houses, except where they followed the precepts of William Morris.

The chimney-pieces of about 1870 designed by W. Burges for his Kensington house might be termed 'Fairy-tale Gothic' but they look like a medieval nightmare! The second illustration is a decorated travesty of the original type of *chimney-hood* (**21**). Less pretentious fire-grates involved the use of 'many shades of gaily-coloured tiles'.

BABY'S HIGH CHAIR
c.1860
(Mahogany & Horsehair)

The helpful hints on utilizing old bedposts, and the applying of wood friezes, come from a 'do-it-yourself' book of the period. The bedposts were considered to be a 'very charming finish to the fireplace', particularly when combined with black beams and white or cream panels on the underside of the canopy.

The addition of applied wood friezes to an existing old beamed room was considered very tasteful, providing that the new wood was camouflaged with greyish-brown stain to match the original timber. The intervening spaces, after being plastered, were covered with a coat of glue, on which was thrown cork-dust or sawdust to give a rough surface; this was then treated with two coats of thick white distemper.

VICTORIAN INTERIOR DECORATION

LIBRARY 1855

"Old bedposts to support half-timbered canopy over a mantelpiece"

CHIMNEY-PIECES c.1870

Tudor

Half-timbered

Classic

APPLIED WOOD FRIEZES

"Fairy tale Gothic"

Gothic

FRUIT BOWL

The interior decoration and furnishing of three different rooms are illustrated on page **91**.

The music room contains a great number of chairs, and numerous potted palms.

An ideal nursery was not too cluttered with furniture so that it could easily be cleaned. The 'do-it-yourself' gentleman advocated a plain, pale sea-green wallpaper; patterned wallpapers were too distracting for young eyes. Blue or mauve were also thought suitable, but definitely not red, pink, yellow, brown or white. The low frieze round the room was decorated with moveable pictures, to avoid monotony. Woodwork should be, with pale green walls, dark sage or olive green. White paint was most impracticable.

A popular ornamental feature was a high frieze inscribed with Improving Mottoes 'in a bold medieval lettering', painted black with scarlet capitals. This practice was not confined to nurseries, but was used in dining-rooms, etc.; one can also imagine the use of admonishing mottoes in servants' quarters.

The typical drawing-room of about 1899 was full to overflowing with draperies, antimacassars, potted palms, occasional tables, and what-nots, and crowded with numerous ornaments and knick-knacks; pictures almost obliterated the walls.

KITCHEN SINK

"MODERN REPRODUCTIONS *of* OLD FIRE-GRATES"

VICTORIAN ROOMS

MUSIC ROOM·1878

NURSERY 1895

S A WAY·WASTE NOT·WANT NOT·PATIENCE

DRAWING ROOM 1899

Victorian Gothic architecture, some of which touched the heights of popularity and the depths of taste, was gradually superseded during the last years of the century by buildings of a new school of thought which combined simplicity with variety, restraint and considerable charm.

The pioneer work of Philip Webb, whose Red House had been a notable landmark in domestic architecture, was followed by R. Norman Shaw who, assisted by Maurice B. Adams and E. J. May, was concerned with Garden City architecture (of which Bedford Park, Turnham Green, London, was the first example, (1876–7). The lead given by these architects was followed by Ernest Newton, George Walton, C. F. A. Voysey, and Sir Edwin Lutyens, to mention but a few.

At first sight, Voysey's house of 1894 seems too startlingly modern to have been built in the Victorian era, with its clean lines, plain hipped roof and remarkable freedom from ornament other than buttresses.

The more fanciful house at Northwood, Middlesex, was designed by R. A. Briggs in 1895. It has large, rounded gables, reminiscent of 17th-century ones (**39, 41**).

The Lutyens house of 1899, built at Witley, Surrey, embodies several features of historical periods of architecture, i.e. gables and massive chimneys, segmental and triangular pediments over its first-floor windows, and classical columns forming the entrance colonnade. In the ground-floor plan of this house, the kitchen and dining room are far from each other, with an almost Georgian disregard for convenience.

The last exterior illustrated was designed about 1900 by George Walton, and built at Shiplake, Oxfordshire. It features a large triangular *pediment* as a gable, and light curved Regency balconies.

The final illustration is of a gallery in a Surrey House, designed by Sir Edwin Lutyens in 1896. Its beams and simple furniture show a taste for something picturesque yet reasonably plain, in reaction from earlier excesses, and is yet another example of how architects favoured styles of construction evolved in bygone centuries.

From this brief survey of man's progress from caves to comfortable houses, via many variations in style, simplicity, pretentiousness, good taste and bad, one conclusion is evident—'there's no place like home'.

This desirable
residence
FOR SALE
Sole agents:
WATTLE & DAUB,
1, GABLE St,
MUCH THATCHING

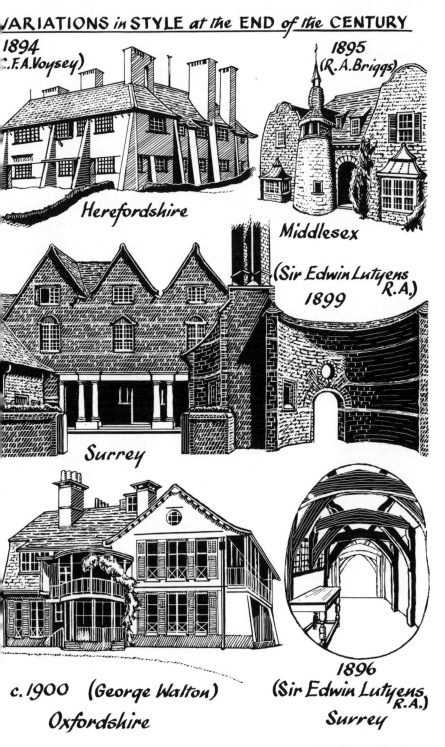

VARIATIONS in STYLE at the END of the CENTURY

1894
(C.F.A.Voysey)

Herefordshire

1895
(R.A.Briggs)

Middlesex

(Sir Edwin Lutyens R.A.)
1899

Surrey

c. 1900   (George Walton)
Oxfordshire

1896
(Sir Edwin Lutyens R.A.)
Surrey

Short Bibliography

ALLEN, A. B., *The Story of your Home*, Faber and Faber Ltd., 1949
—— *18th Century Building*, Barrie and Rockliff Ltd., 1955
BATSFORD, H. and FRY, C., *The English Cottage*, B. T. Batsford Ltd., 1950
BERTRAM, A., *The House*, A. and C. Black, Ltd., 1945
BRAUN, H., *The Story of the English House*, B. T. Batsford Ltd., 1940
BRIGGS, M. S., *The English Farmhouse*, B. T. Batsford Ltd., 1953
DAVIS, F., *Picture History of Furniture*, Edward Hulton and Co. Ltd., 1958
DUTTON, R., *The English Country House*, B. T. Batsford Ltd., 1949
—— *The English Interior*, B. T. Batsford Ltd., 1948
FASTNEDGE, R., *English Furniture Styles from 1500 to 1830*,
    Penguin Books Ltd., 1955
FRANCIS, R., *Looking for Elizabethan England*, Macdonald and Co. Ltd., 1954
—— *Looking for Georgian England*, Macdonald and Co. Ltd., 1952
GARDNER, A. H., *Outline of English Architecture*, B. T. Batsford Ltd., 1949
HOLE, C., *English Home Life, 1500–1800*, B. T. Batsford Ltd., 1947
JEKYLL, G. and JONES, S. R., *Old English Household Life*,
    B. T. Batsford Ltd., 1944–45
JONES, S. R., *English Village Homes*, B. T. Batsford Ltd., 1936
JORDAN, R. F., *A Picture History of the English House*, Edward Hulton
    and Co. Ltd., 1959
JOY, E. T., *English Furniture A.D. 43–1950*, B. T. Batsford Ltd., 1962
OSMOND, E., *Houses* (Junior Heritage Series), B. T. Batsford Ltd., 1956
POTTER, M. and A., *Houses*, John Murray Ltd., 1960
—— *Interiors*, John Murray Ltd., 1957
QUENNELL, M. and C. H. B., *A History of Everyday Things in England* (4 vols.),
    B. T. Batsford Ltd., 1958
—— *Everyday Life in Prehistoric Times*, B. T. Batsford Ltd., 1961
—— *Everyday Life in Roman and Anglo-Saxon Times*, B. T. Batsford Ltd., 1961
SUMMERSON, SIR J., *Architecture in Britain 1530–1830*, Penguin Books Ltd., 1953
TURNOR, R., *The Smaller English House*, B. T. Batsford Ltd., 1952
WARREN, C. H., *English Cottages and Farmhouses*, William Collins,
    Sons and Co., Ltd., 1948
YARWOOD, D., *The English Home*, B. T. Batsford Ltd., 1956

Index

The figures in **bold** type denote the page numbers of illustrations